THE HARP AND THE SWORD

Published and Unpublished Writings and Speeches of

EVANGELINE CORY BOOTH

VOLUME I

Compiled by

JOHN D. WALDRON

Published by

THE SALVATION ARMY

LITERARY DEPARTMENT

USA EASTERN TERRITORY

The Harp and the Sword

Published and Unpublished
Writings and Speeches of

Evangeline Cory Booth

Volume I

by John D. Waldron

ISBN: 089216-095-0

Published by: The Salvation Army
Literary Department
(USA Eastern Territory)
440 West Nyack Road
West Nyack, N. Y. 10994-0635

Printed in the United States of America
First Printing--1992

Table of Contents

Foreword

Commissioner John D. Waldron (R) has once again bent his indefatigable skills as an anthologist to harvest words from the Army's past. Evangeline Booth, daughter of the Founder and fourth General of The Salvation Army, can still speak direct to the heart. Renowned for her oratory no less than for her dramatic personality and charismatic leadership, Eva Booth in her day swayed the emotions to challenge her hearers and to win the hearts of thousands for the Lord. She was an outstanding woman of God.

To have value for us today, words from the past must do more than inform our minds or even warm our hearts. Therefore any Army anthology should not merely lead us into a nostalgia for the past but spur us forward in the cause of Christ.

Eva Booth herself reminds us: "We Salvationists care little for tradition. The past, good as it may have been in conquest and victory, is incomparable with the mighty present and future. It is not to unlock the doors of the barred and finished past that our hearts pine for, but rather to insert the key of unflagging, tireless zeal in the golden lock of opportunity that the future places before us."

Therefore, in commending to your interest and profit General Eva Booth's words, I pray that your zeal and devotion to Christ may be kindled anew. Jesus, who is the same yesterday and forever, is our Lord; our inspiration, today and into the future.

General Eva Burrows

Introduction

When it was suggested by the USA Eastern Territorial Literary Council that we might compile a volume of selected writings by General Evangeline Cory Booth, the task seemed relatively easy.

Her several published books are on my bookshelves, and choice quotations abound, ripe for the compiler's plucking. My modest library, together with my files, offered scores of pages of the writings of this eloquent and dynamic daughter of The Salvation Army's revered cofounders.

Then I began to explore other sources, and I found myself overwhelmed. In The Salvation Army National Archives, then located in Verona, N.J. I discovered six volumes of *War Cry* articles from her 30 years in the United States, with more than 250 articles covering 1966 pages of typescript. Listings alone for other file holdings ran to many pages. Two boxes containing scores of priceless sermon notes kept me enthralled. Boxes of letters and documents provided intimate insight into her mind and heart over the long years of her life, from early officership until past retirement.

The USA Western Territory shared a handwritten set of Training College lectures from her very early years in England and Canada. The George Scott Railton Center in Toronto provided valuable photos and writings from her years of leadership in that territory, as well as important material on Army international affairs and personal glimpses of her children. The School for Officers' Training in Suffern, N.Y. discovered and provided many volumes of typescript not found elsewhere.

Finally, wallowing in thousands of pages of print and pen, I realized that the project had grown far beyond our initial expectations, and the Literary Council proposed that two volumes would be needed to provide even a sampling of the incredible output of her heart and mind.

Months have been spent in reading and deciding what should be left out to keep the books within manageable proportions. We now offer a rather limited distillation of Evangeline Booth's speeches, articles, lectures, sermons, letters, poems and documents. Through them, the reader will catch something of the vision, dynamism and eloquence of this brilliant leader.

A bibliography has been provided for those who are interested in reading further about her life, and this is encouraged. However, we have also provided two brief biographical sketches to introduce her to a new generation of readers: one written at the time of her appointment to Canada, in her very early officership; the other at the time of her promotion to Glory.

The reader is also encouraged to secure the cassette of her voice, in her great lecture, "The World's Greatest Romance." Although recorded in the days of primitive equipment, the quality of her eloquence comes through, and will add a whole new dimension to your understanding of this remarkable woman. The cassettes may be secured from the Trade Departments of the various United States territories.

The compiler's heartfelt thanks are extended to Lt. Colonel William D. MacLean, Literary Secretary, and the

USA Eastern Territory Literary Council, for their guidance and encouragement; to Connie J. Nelson and Susan Sherlock- Mitchem, archivists at the National Archives and Research Center, now located in Alexandria, Virginia; to Major William L. Brown, Director of the George Scott Railton Center in Toronto, and his staff, for valuable assistance; to Colonel Ronald Irwin, for supplying copies of lecture notes; to Major Lorraine Sachs, Librarian at the School for Officers' Training in Suffern, N.Y. for helpful assistance.

At the National Archives, I came across an obscure reference to Evangeline's name, and the quotation forms an appropriate introduction to these volumes. It is taken from undated sermon notes on "Not Well Pleased," in which she lists the books she had read in her youth, including: "*Uncle Tom's Cabin*--(the Eva I was named after). I read it many times over, and it made a mark upon my whole character, making me more careful to be gentle and kind and considerate, most attractive qualities, to those under me--which principles I have endeavored to put into practice until this present day."

J.D.W.

Chapter One

Biographical Information

Commissioner Eva Booth (as a young officer)

The following biographical material was published at the time of her appointment as Territorial Commander in Canada at the age of thirty--very early in her leadership career. The article appeared in The War Cry (Toronto) on May 2, 1896, with the following subtitle:

-A-
TYPICAL WOMAN-WARRIOR
of The
SALVATION ARMY

Converted When Six Years Old--*War Cry* Seller--Captain--A Policeman to the Toughs--Passed Through a Baptism of Rowdyism--Conquered the Torquay Obnoxious Bye-Law--Fought at Whitechurch and Eastbourne--Led London's 21,000 Soldiers to Victory--Wonderful Triumph in New York--Now for Another Chapter of Victory Here.

Commissioner Eva Booth, late pro. tem. in command of the United States forces of The Salvation Army, is the General's fourth daughter.

She was converted at the age of six years, and from her earliest days, in which she was able to take any part at all in the Salvation War, her whole strength and energy has been in some form of work or other for the salvation of the world.

When quite a little miss she used to go out selling *War Crys* on the streets with the women cadets in the first Training Home, carried on under the superintendence of her sister, now Consul Booth-Tucker, and before she was twenty she was able to render great service in that institution in the important work of dealing with the hearts and souls of women who afterwards became Officers in The Salvation Army.

A tremendous storm burst upon The Salvation Army in London in 1885, in consequence of certain actions performed by persons belonging to it, in connection with the terrible Pall Mall Gazette revelations of social vice in the metropolis.

One of these transactions took place in a vicinity where we had a large hall, holding 4,000 people, and there was a dense population of ignorant people of the so-called lower orders of life. Public feeling ran very high against the Army, and in this neighborhood Salvationists were attacked with great violence by mobs when they went out on the streets, and the corps was in a very tight place.

At this juncture, our future Commissioner was appointed to the command as captain, and she went there, having the help of ten or a dozen cadets. Every other house on the street where they lived was a house of iniquity of some form, but before our Commissioner had been in her quarters a fortnight she had been in every house, visiting the people and dealing with them about salvation.

One of the first announcements that she made in the hall was that she was going to be her own policeman inside the building, and that therefore the presence of officers would not be required. This was a bold step in view of the character of the gang of toughs who had been for some little time practically in possession of the hall, but it worked all right, and within a few weeks she had won the respect, and indeed the affection of the whole crowd, and these very men not only preserved excellent order in the hall, but protected Salvationists when they went out on the march. A few months after leaving this corps, when she lay dangerously ill, one of these men pawned his vest in order to buy some hot-house grapes for her.

If any of these lads got into the hands of the police, she would visit them in the lock-ups or prisons and make them feel that they belonged to her as much as she belonged to them. Needless to say, she left a splendid and solid work behind her. Before proceeding further, it might be said that mobs and violence and rowdyism were something to which she had already become well accustomed in various parts of the country, under widely different circumstances, and her courage and boldness on the street were only equalled by her tact and wisdom behind the scenes.

These qualities are supported by a powerful personal love for, and sympathy with, the most needy individuals of the very lowest classes of the people. And there is no man or woman living who could be too filthy, too degraded, too depraved, too vicious, or too desperate, to feel the hand of Commissioner Eva Booth on his or her shoulder, or to look into her dark, lustrous, sympathetic eyes and feel that divine compassion speaks through them.

The Commissioner remained at that corps ten months, and her arduous and endless labors there brought on a dangerous illness, that kept her out of the fight for close on a year. Mrs. General Booth nursed her during the greater part of this time, and the influence of that long, close, loving, personal contact will affect the temporal and eternal destinies of millions.

The next important public conflict was that of Torquay, a health resort in the south of England. The Municipal Council of Torquay deprived, by passing a special bye-law, The Salvation Army of its precious privilege of parading the streets on Sunday with a brass band. This right had been established by a decision of Lord Chief Justice Coleridge, in the Court of the Queen's Bench.

In order to maintain this right, therefore, the procession moved right along by its commander's orders. Officers, bandsmen and soldiers were arrested and cast into prison, but those who remained kept in line and the band played on. There was great excitement in the town, and Commissioner Eva Booth was sent to Torquay, to render her help in fighting the battle through to a victorious finish. She took her place in the parades, when these were attacked by both mobs and police; she personally interviewed and won over the Council. She had the matter taken up by Parliament, and eventually she won by the repeal in Parliament of the obnoxious "bye-law," the right for her army to parade all day if it chose to do so, with its brass band in front and close attendance.

Then again, there was Whitechurch. The issue there was the Army's right to hold open-air meetings. Commissioner Eva came, saw and conquered. The Army held open-air meetings, and is probably holding them yet.

Eastbourne, too. Torquay repeated on a bigger, more bitter, more extensive and much more pertinacious scale. Illness kept the Commissioner out of much of the battle she would have been in if she had been well, but she got round to the houses of the mayor and other leading citizens, and if she did not communicate new truths to them, she placed old facts before them with a force and fervor such as they had never seen before, and have never seen since. She managed to be in the biggest of the series of riots that took place, however, and came through it unharmed, in spite of the fact that a reward of $50 (if we remembered aright) was offered to any man who would knock her down or who could capture her bonnet.

When she received her orders to proceed to New York on her melancholy mission of mercy and love, she was in the midst of arrangements for farewelling from the London "Province" -- When we say that she had 350 field officers, about 200 cadets in training and 21,000 soldiers in her command, it will be seen that she must have great administrative capacity.

Her first two public appearances in America took place on the same day, and before audiences containing a large hostile element. Each meeting, however, resulted in a complete victory. Some of the very people who hissed her at the beginning were cheering her before she finished.

This, too, not because of any plea to their emotions as regarded herself, for the addresses in each case were of an entirely spiritual character, and contained no reference to matters which were then agitating the public mind; but saint and sinner, worldling and backslider, could not but be made aware of the existence of the power of the Holy Ghost in her heart and in her words. Further, it was evident to the most casual observer that she was a woman of intense personal sympathy, large-heartedness, gentleness and kindness.

In the whole history of The Salvation Army probably no officer of any rank ever found himself or herself in any position at all similar to that occupied by her in the first week after her arrival in New York. Yet, during four of those days, she brought about a complete revolution in the feelings of at least 150 officers of various ranks and other persons connected with The Salvation Army in the city, in regard to the position that she assumed under such trying circumstances, and this not by threats or bribes; she fawned on none; she cringed to none; she cajoled none; she flattered none; she begged of none; she offered no inducement to any one. But she accomplished great results simply by the confidence which she inspired in her own integrity and uprightness; in her possession of the Holy Ghost, and the gentle sympathy and Christlike spirit and diplomatic ability which she manifested to those waverers for whom the least allowance would ordinarily be made. In those few days she accomplished a task sufficient for a lifetime in itself, in view of the gigantic interests involved, both present and future, not simply for the United States, but for the whole world.

This colossal task having been accomplished in almost as low a physical condition as it were possible for her to be, what may we expect in the future, when her physical health shall have been restored, and when she shall be able to deal with all the manifold affairs of a vast field, comprising Canada, Newfoundland and Northwest America, in the possession of her full strength of body, mind, heart and soul?

General Evangeline Booth (R)

The following biographical sketch was included in the funeral service of General Evangeline Booth (R) in the Centennial Memorial Temple, New York City, on July 20, 1950.

A unique life of remarkable achievement for God and humanity came to its earthly close with the promotion to Glory of Evangeline Cory Booth, fourth General of The Salvation Army, who on July 17, after months of intense suffering, went to be with her Redeemer and "the saved of the ages." The world she strove all her life to make better mourns the loss of a woman-warrior whose name and deeds will live in all lands through ages to come.

The fourth daughter and seventh child of William Booth, and resembling both in face and spirit her illustrious father, her long career was a saga of tremendous love for the masses as a devoted servant of God; of an inborn dramatic talent and eloquence applied in all its fervor to the cause of a militant gospel; of exceptional administrative gifts, business vision and sane imagination; of travellings that circled the globe; of countless honors including those conferred by Presidents and Kings; of results evident in tens of thousands helped to better things, and thousands lifted from the depths to a high plateau of noble living and useful citizenship.

From Evangeline Booth's earliest days there was bred into the marrow of her bones and injected into the blood of her veins the spirit of crusading religion. The Booth home, her cradle, was the cradle of the Army.

As a babe--she was born on Christmas Day in 1865, the year The Salvation Army was born--she was nurtured on the life-current of the great movement which was even then gathering force to break forth to win the world. As a small child she was rocked to sleep to the tune of songs athrob with the beat of soul-saving passion.

At an age when girls of equal years were thrilling to the dawn of adolescence, she was mounting chairs in the open street and preaching her first sermons and, while still in her teens, was championing the cause of religious liberty, lending the grace and verve of her youth to battles against prejudice and persecution and winning for the then despised Salvationists the right to carry the gospel to the streets.

High-spirited and imaginative, absorbing from the glowing fire of her father's personality the same virile vitamins that energized his life, she ran in the van of the rapidly marching Army and became a figure loved and admired by those Army-makers of the early days.

"White Angel" was the name by which she was known in the London slums, whose abysmal haunts of vice and poverty she explored in the disguise of a ragged flower-vendor or match-girl. "Miss Eva" she was called when serving as Principal of the Army's International Training College, from whence she sent out hundreds of young men and women to live out in far and dark corners of the world her flaming ideals of Salvationism.

Later, as Field Commissioner, she traveled Great Britain extensively, and was obliged to plunge into the riots promoted against the Army at Eastbourne, Torquay and other places.

Then, while still in the full flush of young womanhood, she was dispatched to the American Continent, to become Territorial Commander for Canada and Newfoundland. Here, traveling from coast to coast on errands of inspiration and mercy, her name became a dear and household word. When the human driftwood of the world floated North, in the gold rush of '98, she organized a mission and nursing corps and sent it to the Klondike over the Chilkoot Pass, herself sharing much of the peril and most of the hardships of the pioneers.

In 1904 came transfer to the United States, and the beginning of a thirty-year period as national Leader, during which the rapidity of the Army's onward march, growth and progress was little short of phenomenal. Not only was this so from the standpoint of flesh and blood in soldiery, officers and corps, in finance and in buildings, but in soul-saving and social service usefulness, in public esteem, in community influence and altruistic endeavor. "One of God's best gifts to America" she was called by one of the country's gifted writers.

Despite engrossment with immediate and crying needs in America, however, she kept her sympathies wide as world necessities. Thus, when the Armenian atrocities broke out, she shepherded whole companies of these victims and established them in homes of safety and peace. When famine ravaged India, she gave her eloquent tongue to the cause and sent thousands of dollars for relief. When the news of the great fire and earthquake in Japan was flashed around the world, she took immediate action and raised money for relief on a large scale.

Nor must her broad interest in and valuable contribution to Army policy and government be overlooked. There was hardly any important ruling, regulation or policy of the worldwide Army which did not have the benefit of her shaping hand.

Never in the Army was there a speaker like Evangeline Booth who attracted the professional classes in such large numbers. The phenomenon of the situation was that while lawyers, judges, educators, clergymen and philanthropists came again and again to her meetings, the common people, for whom The Salvation Army primarily exists, increasingly clamored to hear her.

At her busy desk she unfailingly exhibited her fine administrative talents, as quick and as facile in the complicated task of controlling a vast organization as she was in making a happy phrase, powerful utterance, or effective rhetorical flight on the public platform. As one newspaper reporter aptly expressed it: "It was as though a great actress, after thrilling her audience with some powerfully dramatic interpretation, should calmly walk off the stage to the managerial office and proceed to work out the business and technical details of the production in which she was starring. So, during the trying times, she not only drew to the Army a great popular constituency, but also marshaled her forces in such a way as to enable them to present a strong, united front for steady progress in the years to come."

It would be wholly impossible to estimate the vast audiences of her world tours and the value of her labors from "a better world" angle. She traveled throughout the large cities of the North American Continent, the British

Isles, Scandinavia and Europe, Japan, India and the Far East addressing audiences that filled to overflowing the largest public halls to listen to impressive sermons and such celebrated lectures as "The World's Greatest Romance," "Rags," "The Hand of God," and others.

Honors that came to Evangeline Booth make an imposing list. We record but a few: The Distinguished Service Medal, bestowed by the late President Woodrow Wilson; an honorary degree of LL.D. at Columbia University; an honorary degree of M.A. at Tufts College; the Eleanor van Renselaer Fairfax Gold Medal for "eminent patriotic services"; the Vasa Gold Medal by the King of Sweden; and the Gold Medal of the National Institute of Social Science.

At home, General Booth's main preoccupation was music, her favorite instrument being the harp, which she learned to play as a girl and managed to practice sufficiently to play occasionally in public. She wrote the music and composed the words to a number of Salvation Army songs, and a volume of her works, "*Songs Of The Evangel*," was published in 1927 and enjoyed a large circulation throughout the world.

The General wielded an inspired and facile pen. Her books, including *"Towards a Better World," "Love is All,"* and numerous pamphlets and articles are widely read.

During World War I she bought ambulances, commissariat wagons and supplies and rushed them to France; then selected a number of practical, sensible girls to make history with the exploits of The Salvation Army girl--her doughnuts, first-aid, motherly service and practical religion.

Evangeline Booth made the world a better place in which to live. Of that there is no doubt. And because her busy, beneficent life was expended entirely in that direction, the world acclaims her one of the great personalities of all time.

Chapter Two

Catherine and William Booth

Founders of The Salvation Army, United in Wedlock and War

A three-part manuscript written for the centennial year of the birth of Catherine Mumford and William Booth:

A. *The Days of Their Youth*
B. *Oneness of Consecration*
C. *London Surrounded*

From the Library of the School for Officers' Training, Suffern, N.Y., dated April 6-13, 1929. Portions of the manuscript appeared in several Salvation Army publications in various forms.

A. The Days of Their Youth

One hundred years ago, on the 10th of April, 1829, a baby boy was born in Nottingham, England. The skies were aflame with industrial unrest; 10,000 families were living in the throes of a gigantic economic disaster, hunger was imprinted on the faces of men--honest, deserving, hardworking men; and in dimly lighted, poverty-stricken homes mothers and their babes had to exist on what they could pick up for an evening meal.

On the surrounding hills, overlooking the industrial battleground of the great city, lived the wealthy captains of industry, many of whom were indifferent to the sweltering misery of those from whom their princely incomes were pressed.

The city hall was the center of an administration that took no cognizance of suffering. The cry of the oppressed, if uttered by one stung by injustice into revolt, was answered by a ruthless blow. Charity was at a discount. The voice of lawlessness was heard in the land, and the churches appeared to be helpless to ameliorate the lamentable and ghastly social heart-tearing tragedy.

During the same year, under the same lurid skies, in a small village in the county of Derbyshire, a baby girl was born. At that time the same dire poverty prevailed. Agricultural laborers were struggling to rear families on $1.50 per week. Farmers were obliged to fight for their existence under the grinding weight of taxation and the extortionate demand of landlordism. The parents of this little infant were, however, relatively free from such tyranny. Schooled in the faith that enabled them to rise in mind and spirit above the gloomy outlook, they unfalteringly believed that "all things work together for good to them that love God;" and, as they rocked to slumber their treasure in the old-fashioned cradle, they accepted the babe as a sacred and priceless gift from Heaven.

Under such circumstances were born my father and mother, the Founders of The Salvation Army. Romantic and blessed was the manner by which the separate paths of the boy preacher of Nottingham and Catherine Mumford, the ardent student of Ashwarden, came nearer and nearer together, finally to merge into the holy bonds of matrimony and lead to their alliance in an aggressive, militant, conquering Christianity. In the centennial year of these lionhearted apostles, it is neither assuming nor inappropriate that I, their own child and the leader of the movement in this country, should pause to pass in review some of their characteristic features and, from the radiant example they have bequeathed to us, glean learning that will be of profit both to mind and heart. My parents' union, from the hour of their betrothment, in its exemplification of the beauty and sacredness of the marriage covenant, flashes beaconlike across the trend of family life in this age.

For three years Catherine Mumford was exceedingly delicate, confined to her room, often in intense suffering. Her physicians entertained the gloomiest views as to her life being spared. But even in that bitter trial were presaged the stupendous willpower and cheerfulness that distinguished her attitude toward problems that the saints had to encounter. In her affliction she continued her education. She had read the Bible through eight times before she was twelve years old. She familiarized herself with all the Methodist biographies, reveled in revival literature and was an inveterate inquirer after truth on any and every subject of intellectual service. Her worship of truth was a passion.

William Booth, on the other hand, had little time after he left grammar school for a more liberal education. Employers of labor were unrestrained in fixing hours of work. Wages were of the serf standard. My father's first pay envelope contained $3, a stipend for seventy-two hours of work! He grew somber and pessimistic. His idea of a religious life was nothing more than that God was almighty in His power to punish him and that the conclusion of life was Hell for the wicked and Heaven a place for which he could never be good enough.

Yet he inherited from both his parents a strict regard for honesty of purpose, square dealing and an observance of the ordinances of the English Church that held to the verities of Christ, to His atoning sacrifice and to the belief that the world was finally to be brought under the sovereignty of Christ.

Their love for one another, their sacrifice to promote the usefulness of each other, their continued subordination of the lesser pleasure of life, their high experience of Divine fellowship, with their mutual and wholehearted abandonment to the promotion of the salvation of all men, lifted indestructible monuments of holy example the world over.

A Paradox

Two hearts--two wills--two personalities were never more finely blended, never more perfectly attuned to initiate and consummate a worldwide service to humanity than were William and Catherine Booth, the originators and first directors of The Salvation Army.

The story of their union is more than a romance. It was a holy partnership. From the hour that Catherine Mumford, a delicate, timid, yet courageous girl, championed in a London drawing room a temperance recitation by a young Methodist preacher, destined to be her future husband, until her dying entreaty to all men, "Love one another," was winged around the world, the story of their journey through life, their identity of purpose and their union of hearts became such as has been seldom, if ever, recorded.

Yet the early training and domestic circumstances of each were so diverse, so contrary to such a union, as to make it inconceivable that they could ever be joined in the bonds of matrimony or become leaders of an undreamed of spiritual conquest. Their whole story is one of love and religion interwoven into a beautiful pattern of enduring fellowship.

Differences in Disposition

While there was marked diversity in their dispositions, they were akin in their adherence to high spiritual standards. My father was in altruism what Napoleon was in war--a man of destiny. My mother arrived at conclusions through mental reflection and sound reasoning.

His mind, like the lightning, leapt to its objective. Her mind was illumined by the candle of truth and philosophy.

His love for my mother, as a maiden, a bride and a lifelong partner, in peace and war, poverty or enough was a profound, impassioned, undeviating devotion. Her love for him was an ever-flowing tide of unbreakable continuity, a sacred service and inspiring passion.

He was a warrior of the field, a man of action, intensely practical in thought and deed. She was a student of moral and spiritual categories, with the prescience of a prophetess, foreseeing The Salvation Army commingled for a worldwide awakening to the teaching of Jesus Christ. Unperturbed in a storm, her feet were immovable on the bridge.

He was an Evangelical Trojan, living and having his being in immediate and decisive spiritual conquests. She was metaphysical, serene, calm, like the night stars.

He organized, stimulated, enacted laws and regulations for his troops. She created an atmosphere of spirituality, he an atmosphere of advancement.

Their Pole Star

William Booth was a General eager for action, determinedly set on progress. But both were alike in their ever-bounding love of Christ. The life of each was surrendered for all time to the salvation of souls and their consecration was uniform. This gave to both perfect union of motive, harmony of spirit, intensity of service. The uplift of man, spiritually and morally, was the Pole Star of their world.

While William Booth, martial and militant, was contending with the offscouring of misery and crime in the slums, Catherine was challenging the veneered paganism of the erudite of the same city.

While he would be upholding the Cross before the masses in a theater, or hall, or on the public thoroughfare, she--her philosophic and scientific mind strengthening rather than weakening her faith in Jesus Christ as her Lord and Savior--with voice and pen, would be grappling with the questionings of the doctrinaire and calling upon the churches to leap from their slumbers, forsake their vanities and follow in purity the Christ of the Cross.

With more than the average sickness, trial, sorrow and separation consequent upon the high calling to which they had surrendered their lives, and with it the absence of the many felicities that lighten the burdens of home and family, not a shadow of distrust ever crossed the heart or home of William and Catherine Booth. They were the Robert and Elizabeth Browning of Christian Evangelism.

My mother, with the infinite patience of genius, was the chief trainer and director of the minds and hearts of her eight children. My father was the daring, almost ruthless commander who called early from the cloister of a domestic shrine these same children to shoulder the Gospel musket and man the trenches in the offensive and defensive war being waged against debauchery, squalor and sin. Together they knelt at the same altar of sacrifice and offered their children to God. They were as two threads of totally different shade woven into one beautiful fabric, working out a pattern for all men, through all time, to look upon and imitate.

Crusaders

The battle element in their religion brought them into conflict with the religious Sanhedrins of their day. It was not strange that the world opposed them, for their battle was against the vicious interests of organized and legalized crime. Their mission was the alleviation of sorrow, the healing of the broken in heart. Their battlefield was the holes and haunts of the wretched, their story the all-redeeming Gospel of Jesus Christ. They preached in alley, street and slum. To purchase that right they were forced to witness innocent women condemned to prison. They had to meet the scowl of a religious *laissez-faire*! It was *lese-majeste* to beat a drum! It was "Corybantic Christianity" to thump a tambourine! It was a crime to impair the traditional dignity of military etiquette by adopting military nomenclature! It was an offense against good taste to publish a paper with such a militant title as *The War Cry*.

Ridicule and persecution were inevitable. Every movement based on the teaching of Christ has at its inception encountered opposition. My mother, an invalid almost from her childhood and the carefully nursed flower of a secluded Christian family, with her intensely refined disposition, mentally recoiled when called to face the turmoil and violence of the "baser sort." But, warrior and saint as she was, she would take her place in the front line of the combat. In all the vicissitudes of life and in all the ebb and flow of battle she was the same--a reformer, a Christian crusader, a warrior and a saint.

Prophetess

A conception of the nature and depth of their unity in wedlock, with its supreme concept of fidelity to Christ, is best derived from their letters to each other.

Fortunately, volumes of these still exist. The following extracts, for the present purpose, are selected at random. There is scarcely a line in the mass preserved that does not disclose the unbreakable links of the mystic fellowship that bound them to the ideal of winning the world for their Redeemer.

Marriage Problems

Their days of contemplation of marriage were passed in a spirit of thoughtfulness and prayer. Before she called him her "precious William," Miss Mumford wrote:

> "My dear Friend:
> I have been spreading your letter before the Lord, and earnestly pleading for a manifestation of His will to your mind."

Then, chiding him for an undertone of pessimism and fear, even "melancholy and despair," observable in one of William Booth's letters at this time, this gifted, whole-souled woman expostulated with him in these searching, kind and direct sentences:

> "Don't give way to such feelings for a moment. God loves you. He will sustain you. The thought that I should increase your perplexity and cause you any suffering is almost intolerable. I am tempted to wish that we had never seen each other. Do try to forget me as far as the remembrance would injure your usefulness or spoil your peace. If I have no alternative but to oppose the will of God or trample on the desolations of my own heart, my choice is made. 'Thy will be done' is my constant cry. I

care not for myself, but, oh, if I make you to err, I shall never be happy again!"

It is difficult to say whom most to admire--the Methodist preacher, absorbed in soul-saving engagements, away from the home of the woman he loved and somewhat perplexed as to whether he was quite right in indulging the hope that Catherine Mumford might become his partner; or that tender woman-heart, also possessed of a lofty and pure affection for a man who answered her ideals of a true Christian and a devotee of her Master's eternal aim.

One thing is certain. From the day their eyes spoke of a hidden admiration for each other, they would not allow even that sacred touch of an ancient lyre to divert them from the contemplation of marriage without the most importunate plea for Divine guidance. This is a typical paragraph in the majority of my mother's letters:

"If -- Well, We Shall Have Peace"

"Again I commend you to Him. It cannot, shall not, be that you shall make a mistake. Let us besiege His Throne with all the power of prayer."

In such an attitude of mind and heart, how could a mistake occur? When all was clarified and these souls, these lovers of Calvary, were of one mind, this is how Catherine Mumford with faithful spirit gazed into the future:

"If, indeed, we are the disciples of Christ, in the world we shall have tribulation, but in Him and in each other we shall have peace. If God chastises us by affliction, in either mind, body or circumstances, it will only be a mark of our discipleship and, if borne equally by us both, will not only be softened but sanctified, and we shall be enabled to rejoice that we are permitted to drain the bitter cup together."

We know--all the world knows--the issue of that union, sanctified by an intelligent consecration of every talent they possessed to the service of humanity. They loved each other and their love was born of God.

B. Oneness of Consecration

To the traveler flying over the lakes of Switzerland, sparkling like pearls of wonderment, the majestic crowns of the Alps make their varied appeal from differing vantage points.

One observer will lose sight of everything except the proud, snowcapped splendor of Mont Blanc. Another will be enticed by the less pretentious beauty of the lower ranges.

In like manner the qualities that distinguish the genius and accomplishments of my parents are subject to individual preference. But those who came in contact with them, whether at home or abroad, were alike impressed with the completeness, the oneness, the self-effacement, yet fullness of joy, in their devotion to Christ and the world for which He died.

How severe the test to which my mother was subjected when my father was compelled through sickness, already overtaxed with the care of a young family, to leave the charge of a Methodist Church at Gateshead, England! How cheerfully she endured the test is revealed in a letter to her mother, to whom she also reveals her secret feelings as a minister:

> "William, of course, is very pleased and says he felt quite comfortable at home minding the bairns, knowing who was supplying his place...If I had but time to study and write, I should not fear now; but I must be content to do what I can, consistently with my home duties, and leave the future to the Lord...I continue my visitations among the drunkards...
>
> "I have had ten pledged men to begin with, most of whom have been much addicted to drink for years."

Kitchen and Pulpit

To my mother, innately of a retiring disposition, notoriety was exceedingly painful. Speaking of a deputation that was urging her to undertake additional public service, she said:

> "I told them it was easy talking, etc. They little know what it cost me, nor anybody else either,

except the Lord. You see, I cannot get rid of the care and management of things at home, and this sadly interferes with the quiet necessary for preparation; but I must try to possess my soul in patience, and to do all in the kitchen, as well as in the pulpit, to the glory of God. The Lord help me!"

Another remarkable trait was the constant identity of her own with her husband's all consuming passion. At the zenith of his success in Gateshead they resolved, should their Conference fail to give them a roving commission for soul-saving service, to sever their connection with the Conference and go out into the more promising field of itinerant evangelism.

Every "catch" they had hitherto made, following a "launch" out into the deep, had served the more to convince them that, moored to the shore by ecclesiastical chains, they might "toil all night"--night after night--and take little or "nothing." Believing themselves to have been called of God to be "fishers of men," they contested the right of the Church to mark off a "preserve" and put an interdict on "free fishing." She would, in their judgment, be untrue to her calling in the raising of a restrictive bar against the great commission: "Go ye into all the world, and preach the gospel to every creature." Within sight of the church vestibule were harvests to be gathered from infernos of degradation. My mother's visits to the slums--habitations often less than fit for dog kennels--had plunged her into the physical and spiritual Gethsemanes. The Mahomet theory of going to the mountain when the mountain failed to come to him was dawning on the General.

The Fiat of Independence

His Church Conference cast the vote that determined his destiny. His request for the wider field of labor was discussed with comparative disapproval. When, finally, the assembly refused to sanction his appeal--although at a previous sitting it had been practically conceded--proposing a compromise unfavorable to my father's desire, the righteous indignation of Mrs. Booth, strong in the sincerity of their united motives, found vent in a scene which is graphically described by Commissioner Booth-Tucker in his life of "Catherine Booth, the Army Mother:"

"When the compromise was carried it was more than Mrs. Booth could endure. She had been sitting at a point in the gallery, from which she and her husband could interchange glances. It had been with difficulty that she had restrained her feelings hitherto while listening to the debate. But at this stage she was overcome with indignation. She felt that Dr. Cooke had sacrificed their cause in the interests of peace rather than righteousness. But for his suggested compromise she believed that they would have carried the day with a triumphant majority. He had deserted them in the very hour of victory, carrying with him a number of those who had already voted in favor of the appointment. But she would be no party, even by her silence, to the compromise. It was one of those supreme moments when rules and regulations are forgotten and the heart out of its own fullness acts upon the promptings and inspiration of the hour.

"Rising from her seat and bending over the gallery, Mrs. Booth's voice rang through the Conference, as she cried to her husband, 'Never!'

"There was a pause of bewilderment and dismay. Every eye was turned toward the speaker in the gallery. The idea of a woman daring to utter her protest, or to make her voice heard in the Conference, produced little short of consternation. It was a sublime scene, as, with flushed face and flashing eyes, she stood before the audience. Decision, irrevocable and eternal, was written upon every feature of that powerful and animated countenance. Her 'Never' seemed to penetrate like an electric flash through every heart.

"One, at least, in that assembly responded with his whole soul to the call. Mr. Booth sprang to his feet and waved his hand in the direction of the door. Heedless of the ministerial cries of 'Order! Order!' and not pausing for another word, they hurried forth, met and embraced each other at the foot of the gallery stairs and turned their backs upon the Conference. Thus, amid a deluge of heartbreaks and disappointments...The Salvation Army ark was launched."

Happiness in a Wilderness

Weighed in the scales of personal comfort, the resolve of my parents was foolish. It was tantamount to a disregard of the first obligation of parents. As the General admitted in his formal letter of resignation (dated July 18, 1861):

"I know what I am sacrificing and I know I am exposing myself and those I love to loss and difficulty. But I am impelled to it by a sense of duty to souls, to the Church and to God. Were I to quail and give up for fear of the difficulties which just now appear to block my path, I feel sure that I should in the future reproach myself with cowardice in the cause of my Master, and that even those who differ with me in opinion would say that I was not true to the professions I made in the Conference, when I said, 'I had offered myself to the Lord, for this work, if I went forth without a friend and without a shilling!'"

My mother, writing to her parents the day after the event, declared: "I have not felt happier for three months."

In the United States, fashioned and welded in revolt and in whose Constitution, which the late Lord Bryce has declared to be the greatest declaration of political faith in the history of the world, are written the imperishable words that every man has the right to worship God according to the dictates of his own conscience, the step taken by my brave mother and father--isolating them from all social contacts--must command the veneration of every citizen. It was a protest against compromise with a sacred obligation; it was obedience to the noblest promptings to which the human mind can respond; it was the acceptance of the will of God with loss and poverty and hardship as the only apparent emolument.

It is plain that the hand of God was shaping the character of each. He planned this perfect combination, honoring each with gifts which, while widely diverse, were essentially one in the creation of The Salvation Army, a "building not made with hands."

In this Centenary let us raise our voices again in praise to God for the wedlock that was to link forever not only two souls as one, but nation to nation, continent to continent and race to race, in the bonds of the Gospel of our Lord and Savior Jesus Christ.

Universal Gain

All nations have derived benefit from the union of William Booth and Catherine Mumford. The world knows and has paid tribute to their greatness: as Founders of the Army, as leaders of men of all nations, as philanthropists for all people, as organizers of all phases of service, as servants of the living God.

But only their children can the more exhaustively appraise their true worth, their spiritual elevation, their magnetic power as parents and as examples. In my earliest years the beauty and luster of their Christian living was the light upon my way. It will shine brightly and even more brightly until the end of the journey. Their courage and their unflinching contention for right, so often with great material loss, always and every time proved to us in our childhood and through our maturing years that righteousness must triumph. Our awakening souls witnessed the truth of their teaching that His grace was sufficient by their united and unfailing cheerfulness and trust amid the fury of bitter storms; by my father, in his optimistic and relentless pushing of the battle to the gate, by his fearless example and by the fires of his own soul spurring his people to spend themselves to the limit; by my mother, in her eloquent and philosophical reasoning, silencing the criticism voiced by the specious oracles of conventional Christianity and, by her trenchant pen, defending women's right to preach the Gospel of Jesus Christ and liberating her sex from ages of prejudice. With our eyes resting upon these holy things we grew up to years of understanding.

It was said to me the other day by one who knew my father well, "The General was quick to anger, was he not?" I replied, "Perhaps. I could not tell unless I knew the circumstances under which he evinced anger or wrath!" I have seen, when he was stirred by some act of injustice, something like the wrath of God on his face. But his anger always had a just cause, and one was always the better for his reproof, were it of a sharp nature or otherwise, for it was ever tempered by the justice and the mercy of the heart of the true man. When he was sorely grieved, the expression of his displeasure was not the lightning that destroyed, it was the fire that refined. You were a wiser man for it. Then, too, his anger was counterbalanced a hundredfold by his swiftness to forgive. He was the quickest man to forgive I have ever known, read about, or heard of--or that I ever expect to. Everybody loved him. Men loved him without stopping to consider whether he was lovable or not--whether it would promote the interests of their kindred or not; without stopping to weigh pros and cons, a nameless intangible something which, like a magnet, drew the hearts of the whole world to him. You loved him just because you could not help it. This, linked to his abiding sympathy toward the weak and helpless, drew peoples of all nations to acknowledge the glory of our Blood and Fire Banner.

A Napoleonic Strategist

The history of The Salvation Army bears in a special sense the imprint of the overwhelming mastermind of its Founder. His personality attracted the attention of a wakening Church, and stalwart Christians like R. C. Morgan, Samuel Morley, T. A. Denny and Henry Reed, saw in the Christian Mission--the vanguard of The Salvation Army--the first attempt since the early days of Methodism to organize an unremitting effort for the salvation of souls.

My father gathered around him roughly polished artisans and their wives, sanctified for service, even unto death. As stones whizzed through the air while they preached the gospel in city alleyways, upholders of the law stood by and encouraged the mob to do violence. Such were his ministers--men and women who lived in "the Light of God." They wept when their pleas and prayers failed to bring men to repentance; they held themselves in readiness either in sickness or in health, to do anything, go anywhere, suffer, toil and even die for the salvation of the people.

There was no training college in those early days. The streets, lanes and alleys of the great cities were our drill ground as well as our battle area. My father's unsurpassed passion for the souls of men, his dauntless courage and his unquenchable optimism formed the vat which gave the coloring to all his followers. In nothing was his daring and foresight exhibited so much as in his work in leasing and purchasing buildings purely for soul-saving.

It was not till his fifth mammoth salvation hall was opened near to Mayfair that *Punch* began to take notice of "William Booth, with the big bass drum," and the girl with the Quaker-like bonnet. *Punch*, lest any American citizen miss the meaning of this reference, is the national wit newspaper, unsullied by "suggestions," clever and perfect in syntax, matchless in artistic skill. Mention in its columns was the direct and sure route to fame!

When General Booth was first "glorified" in its pages, he said to his son, Bramwell, "At last the tide is turned. We shall now be in danger of becoming too respectable!"

C. London Surrounded

The Founder of The Salvation Army, by master strokes of initiative, proved himself a strategist.

He honeycombed the heart of London, in a semi-circle, with citadels of salvation. The first of these was the historic Congress Hall, seating 6,000 people and lying athwart the poverty-stricken districts of Homerton and Hackney. This adventure attracted the attention of the newspapers and in honor of the event they ceased to use quotation marks when mentioning the name of the General. The next important achievement was the capture of the Grecian Theater, one of the most popular places of amusement of the lower type. The Grecian would be considered on Broadway today not at all a place of contemptible dimensions. With a saloon, dancing and serenading grounds and an auditorium capable of accommodating 5,000 people, London laughed at the assumption that a praying and singing band of semi-dervishes could attract a hundred people.

But people were unaware of the psychological vision possessed by the General. He chose for the venture not one of his most cultured staff, or some one from the ranks of the ordinary field officers. Hoxton was the Mecca of East End knuckle-dusters and the City Road the rendezvous of the second-story man. An officer called Stonehill, with a voice that would and did wake from the dead many a spiritually interred Lazarus and an expert in the "noble art of self-defense," was appointed pastor. The night the Grecian's capture was celebrated fully 10,000 people failed to find admission. The newspapers played on the favorite lute of satire. A wave of emotionalism they styled it. That wave swept the world!

Regent Hall, known best as "The Rink," has today a brass band of exceptional talent that has had the honor of playing many times in the grounds of Buckingham Palace, always with royal sanction and sometimes by express royal command. With the opening of Regent Hall, an old skating rink, situated in the heart of the West End of London, the metropolis was environed with salvation and, when attacked by the obviously superficial query, "Will it last?" the General of this holy war would reply "Ask Spurgeon (the great nonconformist pastor of the Tabernacle) who declared that the presence of The Salvation Army in London saved the city the expense of maintaining 5,000 extra policemen." The mainspring of this stupendous moral force was found in the tirelessly working brain and the burning love and zeal of my father.

William Booth, LL.D

My father never lingered by the way. The cry of souls rang in his ears like the SOS calls of ships. The Salvation Army crossed the English Channel and swept the seas; in far distant lands there was daring enterprise, the same commanding power and holy determination to fight back the enemies of the souls and bodies of men.

Green, in his history of Methodism, gives that cult the credit of raising the moral standard of England, and he even held the view that its saturation of the masses with the Gospel teaching of John Wesley had much to do with the renaissance of learning and poetry. From the encomiums that poured upon my father when presented with the Freedom of the City of London and, afterwards, the honorary degree of LL.D of the University of Oxford, it became clearer that The Salvation Army was of indispensable value to the welfare of the land.

A Vacant Chair

But a shadow fell. The "Mother of The Salvation Army"--that sheet anchor of my father's turbulent and yet victorious life, mother of his much beloved children, counselor in war, solace and inspiration in peace, companion in all things pertaining to their life and eternity--fell in battle with the sword in her hand.

By the side of the sea in a little bungalow-like cottage, she fought a deadly disease for nearly two years, but never once would she permit her lionhearted helpmate to desert his duty as General of the Army or his Heaven-sent message to dying souls. "They are waiting for you, William, dear," she would say as he would hand his little valise to his secretary and tear himself away to some foreign land. Shall we ever know--I mean the world as well as Salvationists--what that blow meant to my father? Shall we ever realize what followed in that sick room?

For it was there that the "Darkest England Scheme" was devised. In her room, whilst the waters leapt upon the great rocks, despite her sufferings, she would speak about the principles underlying the formation of shelters for the homeless, workshops for human castaways, refuges for wayward girls, homes for unmarried mothers and all the intricate arrangements grouped under the conception of salvaging broken men and women. Her sick room also became a sacred shrine for veterans in the war.

The parting from her beloved, her "most precious William," "her darling husband," and her beloved boys and girls was a dark day. We were called to her bedside and, although for two long years we had expected it, it seemed incredible to have to associate death with her. She had been so vital to us, such a forerunner, so triumphant in her individual warfare, so glorious in her self-forgetting service for others. How could we reconcile her splendid powers with the terror of dissolution? But death was there. We could see its gray shadow falling upon the precious face.

The terrible suffering which had racked her was suddenly assuaged, she was restful--quiet. She was beyond all speech. Her eyes, shining with the brilliancy of stars to the last, passed from one child to another and, then became fixed upon my father's face--that face which had been the one face of all the world to her. It seemed that she had an agreement with my father that if speech left her before death came and if she realized that Christ was with her in the Valley she would wave her handkerchief to let her husband and her children know that all was well with her at the last. Rallying her remaining strength, she raised it up-up-up, once, twice, thrice. Only an instant it remained uplifted; then the worn, tired arm sank, but still the hand was raised and, when that could no longer uphold, her thin forefinger moved back and forth, then fell, the eyes closed, and she was asleep. But we received the message; we knew that she had found in the Valley the One for whom she had looked, and that upon His breast He had given "His beloved sleep."

Mysterious? Yes, and no! London thought so. Old evangelists of pre-Army days felt that the Army would lose part of its crown. The press extolled her virtues and acknowledged her as the forerunner of a new charter of women's liberty. As her cortege passed the London Stock Exchange, Jew and Gentile, Catholic and Protestant closed their places of business, and many wept. The poor came to her bier and wreathed her casket with tears and flowers.

But one man, dignified in bereavement, strong in faith in the divinity of his call to stand by the Army Flag in all weathers, in all reverses and successes, thus expressed himself:

"There has been taken away from me the delight of my eyes, the inspiration of my soul, and we are about to lay all that remains of her in the grave. I have been looking right at the bottom of it here, and calculating how soon they may bring and lay me alongside of her, and my cry to God has been that every remaining hour of my life may make me readier to come and join her in death, to go and embrace her in life in the Eternal City!

"I have never turned from her these forty years for any journeyings on my mission of mercy but I have longed to get back, and have counted the weeks, days and the hours which should take me again to her side. And now she has gone away for the last time! What, then, is there left for me to do? Not to count the weeks, the days and the hours which shall bring me again into her sweet company, seeing that I know not what will be on the morrow, nor what an hour may bring forth. My work plainly is to fill up the weeks, the days and the hours, and cheer my poor heart as I go along with the thought, that, when I have served my Christ and my generation according to the will of God--which I vow this afternoon I will, to the last drop of my blood--then I trust that she will bid me welcome to the skies, as He bade her."

Within a few months after the death of my mother, where do we find the Founder? Among the Kaffirs and Zulus of South Africa, preaching righteousness and redemption through Jesus Christ; among the gold fields of

Western Australia; preaching of Calvary to little groups of Cingalese in the jungle of Ceylon and the villagers of Gujerat, finishing with a flying trip to the place of our Lord's nativity, where people of all nations and creeds and tongues were represented among those seeking their way to the Cross.

Apostle-like Journeys

This first world tour of the General put a new spark of holy ambition into the councils of the Army. It revealed to the leaders the adaptability of the Army to establish itself among all peoples and tongues. It showed that a fearless and sincere proclamation of the mercy purchased by Jesus Christ on Mount Calvary was responded to by thousands who were ignorant of the Scriptures. It gave new vision to officers in all lands as to the destiny of the Flag. It made the internationalism of the Army become clearer and dearer. It was felt that its strength was not in mere denominational unity, but in the exhibition in personal sacrifice of the impulse and passion to preach Jesus Christ and to work out in their lives the meaning of Calvary, and drill men and women everywhere as soldiers in a great warfare. It was the beginning of a new era.

In the Valley of Darkness

And so it was to the day when another shadow fell upon the Army, the day when the oculist declared that my father was blind. But even that did not daunt him. "Blind?" he spoke, softly but not complainingly. "But," he added, "Doctor, I shall see God. I have tried to serve my Lord with two eyes, and now I am called upon to serve Him without them. So let it be. His will be done. Milton, blind seer, saw into the future, and saw things of the past in a new light. Dear old Ranger (the Army's lawyer), got his LL.D from Oxford and never was able to read it. He was blind from his youth up."

But the Founder was always ready to submit his confidence to the test. He went back to the battlefield, back to cheer his troops and warn the rebels against leaving God out of their lives. Led by the hand of one of his trusted aides to his beloved Congress Hall, the old fire of a deathless purpose would shine through his sightless eyes. Facing a dark, dark blank, the old warrior would address the auditorium as if he beheld an Army too numerous to count and a people all aflame with a full resolve to renounce all worldly ease and go forth to a new conquest for the Cross. Only those whose spirits were tuned to the fading but triumphant music of the grand warrior's march to the River could interpret the high note of victory that reverberated through the old Colosseum-like building. His last words in the temple were worthy of the greatness of the event:

> "I want you to promise me that when my voice is silent and I am gone from you, you will use such influence as you may possess with the Army to do more for the homeless of the world. The homeless

men! Mind! I am not thinking of this country only but of all lands."

Till the last the poor, the most abandoned, were mirrored in his soul. And what of the present? Other founders have gone up higher. Other warriors have yielded their swords for the crown of righteousness. Suppose we take a glance at their lives and ask ourselves the question with which the Founder so frequently closed his salvation mass meetings--"What have you done with your life?"

Many who read this will recall seeing the prophet himself, standing before thousands of our American soldiers, his flowing beard, his magnificent physique and his eyes aflame, compassionate and so solicitous for an answer that would cheer the very source of Heaven's power, the heart of Jesus--giving emphasis to his own reply, "My Lord, but for my sins washed from the book of Thy remembrance and a life driven to despair but for Thine ineffable grace, my life would have been barren and useless; but Thou didst save my soul, when a lad of seventeen, and I come to place before Thy Throne the fruit of it--The Salvation Army." And so in my father's name I ask again, "What are you doing with your life?"

What They Did With Their Lives

Jesus Christ was born in a manger, crucified on Mount Calvary and oh, wonder of wonders--was crowned the Sovereign of the world and its only Redeemer.

Paul, the Christian Apostle to the Gentile world, unfurled the Flag of Calvary in pagan Rome and saved Europe and Asia from moral corruption.

Martin Luther obliterated the spiritual darkness from Europe and revealed to it a clearer vision of faith as taught in the New Testament.

John Wesley resurrected the teaching of holy living or what he termed "experimental godliness," at a time when Great Britain was steeped in religious formality and by his converts bequeathed to the world the Methodist communions.

Duff, Moffat, Livingstone and an army of martyrs and missionaries radiated paganism with the "Light of the World."

William Booth, a Nottingham clerk, who gave his life to God at the age of seventeen, dissatisfied with the religious conventionality of the day, developed into a fiery evangelist and traveled the world, winning hundreds of thousands of souls for his Savior. He unfurled the Blood-and-Fire Banner that has waved for the help of more bodies and souls of men than any religious flag that has ever flown.

Catherine Booth, a frail, delicate girl, reared in a haven of spiritual decorum and grace, was converted at twelve. At the age of twenty-six she married William Booth, and with him founded The Salvation Army. Her sublime faith in God, her unbounded compassion for the sinning, sorrowing and poor, her resonant voice as preacher and lecturer, her intellectual powers as a philosopher and author, carried her influence and fame to the uttermost parts of the earth. She was carried to her grave by her converts, and the City of London stood still as the cortege passed by. She is sacredly named today, "The Mother of The Salvation Army."

What Others Did

Pharaoh sought to destroy a race, and in trying to do so he and his warriors perished in the Red Sea, while the pursued became the "people of God."

Nebuchadnezzar the Great corrupted his court, was bereft of reason and sentenced by a righteous God to live as a beast of the field.

Julius Caesar, wading through blood to wear the imperial robes of Rome, ignobly died at the hands of an assassin.

Alexander the Great, sweeping across Eastern Europe, conquering and destroying, laid waste the cultured civilization of Greece, ravaged its altars and slew its priests. Such was the work of the man called by history "great." Saturated with carnage and destruction, all hope for millions of his fellow-men was crushed under the heel of his unparalleled tyranny. And yet, gazing confounded at the sun in all its glory, he wept because there were no more worlds to conquer and died an ignominious death.

Cardinal Wolsey drank from golden goblets. He supped from bowls of silver. Fortunes flashed like stars from the sapphires on his fingers. Honors and dignities were conferred upon him; but, arrogant and imperious, he dared to act in defiance of the royal will and at the last, stripped of his honors and driven from the court, he died in deserved disgrace. Bitterly enough did he say:

> "Would that I had served my God as diligently as I have served my king! He would not in my old age have left me naked to mine enemies."

Louis XIV, who proudly declared *L'etat c'est moi,* bewitched by the charms of his mistress, the Marquise de Maintenon, stained his hands with the blood of the saints, established an unparalleled system of espionage for the maintenance of his own despotism, debased his court by nameless scandals and died in dishonor, leaving France to be swept by the deluge of the red revolution.

Now, My People, What Will You Do With Your Lives?

My Staff: I appeal to you. In this centennial year I long to see you inspired as never before by the conquests of my beloved father. Our great America needs leadership after his similitude. You know where the secret of his power resided. Seek for more and more of that power to fill your own hearts and to be made manifest in your own lives.

My Field Officers: I appeal to you. Yours is the key position of the battle. I ask you to re-read and pray over the story of my beloved father's life. He was the first field officer of The Salvation Army. He battled forlorn hopes, he struggled in poverty, he fought opposition, he faced prison and the fires of ridicule and satire; but he conquered.

Today he is sitting, according to the Divine promise, "With Me in My Throne, even as I also overcame, and am set down with My Father in His throne."

My Local Officers: I appeal to you. You are the elders of our Israel, the guardians of our name and upholders of our laws. You are the candles of our temple nearer to the homes and workshops of our land than any other of the commissioned officers. I want you to profit by all that is embraced in this centenary celebration and give the lead for every soldier to follow. May God give you fresh oil for your lamps and a new power to carry the salvation gospel to every home in your city!

My Bandsmen: I appeal to you. Laurels of victories shine on your instruments, earth and Heaven being the richer by your talent, sacrifice and constancy of effort. But, comrades, there are still many dark places in America. In one city, I am reliably informed, are 15,000 places organized to defy the law and distribute the curse of modern civilization. May you, each and all of you, swell the grand strain of this centennial year and let the note of a holy war be heard in slum and hall, in the meeting resorts of the common folks, to all who pass by, to whom "'tis nothing that Jesus should die."

My Company Guards and Corps Cadets: On you rests, to a large degree, the Army of tomorrow. To you I look for brave, whole-hearted, single-minded officers. I appeal to you, to read carefully and prayerfully what I may say from time to time about this call to American Salvationists to serve God and the flag as my father did and, if he were alive, as he would expect from you.

And for myself, I appeal to you all: First, and all important, for your prayers. Without the upholding hands of Aaron and Hur the battle with Amalek might have ended in defeat. You are my armor-bearers, my eyes, my ears, my counselor in war and my leaders in the heart of the fight. Pray, pray for me: that I may have wisdom and insight to the secret will of God; that I may have strength to bear the burden and heat of the day and that I may be a leader in the truest sense of the word, a leader in action, a leader in sacrifice, a leader in toil, a leader in triumph.

Life today is one of action. Progress is progressive. The old lazy idea of leaving the most difficult task until the millennium is the idea of petrified fossils. We must fly; no longer run. I must today work the works of Him that sent me, win many more souls, inspire more soldiers and by God's grace quicken the life and spirit of the war; and to you I turn for that cooperation and confidence that will guarantee that we shall see greater things than have yet been done in the name of our Supreme General in Chief and Lord of all.

My Wandering Comrades: I appeal also to you. Many of you I know by name, and many by happy personal association under the flag. "Demas hath forsaken me" was not spoken by Paul in anger. There is infinite feeling and the tenderest entreaty in the words. In the same spirit I appeal to you, in the spirit of love, hope and faith. Come back, comrades! Come back! In this appeal I voice the cry of thousands of old and fond comrades. Come back! Come back to your long closed Bible. Come back to the old joyous songs. Come back to the blessed happy gatherings. Come back to hearts that have never ceased to pray for you. Come back to Christ who shed His Blood to save you! Come back and march with us to Glory! Come back! Come home!

My Mother, the Army's Mother

A manuscript found in the Library of the School for Officers' Training, Suffern, N.Y. Printed, in edited form, in various Salvation Army publications, including The War Cry (New York) April 9, 1938; and The War Cry (Chicago) May 13, 1939. "Some handwritten marginal notes (where legible) have been included in the final copy."

Sitting before her pictured face it is impossible for me to realize the years that divide us--that her dwelling in the Eternal City separates me from the blessing of her bodily presence.

It is vain to recall the many momentous happenings in which she has not shared; the marvelous development of the movement she left bereaved; the changes which have come to individuals; or the progress of the world since the grass of Spring first greened on her grave.

Her grave speaks only of the last farewell. For, wonderful mother, you are as inseparable from my life as ever! Even death, the arch-dissolver of earth's strongest ties, cannot break the bonds by which thou art bound to my heart and, looking into thy face, I read again the lovely things--the holy things--you wrote upon the pages of my memory. And I thank Thee, Lord, our Savior, for that most potent gift of memory! That which likens us unto a god in its power to make as nonexistent spaces and times, and to bring out of the furtherest recesses of the past into the last second of the present faces and forms and happenings and conditions--quicker than the clock can tick or our lips can speak.

There are few things more wonderful than the power of memory. It surely must be accounted one of the most striking capacities with which God has endowed man--this vital tenacity of the mind which holds to subjects and things and creatures and places that away back in the past have come into our lives and, bringing them through the years, gives them to us today preserved in their entirety.

We change. Everything about us changes. Our homes change, our cities change, our countries change, our handwriting changes, even our bodies change; our straight shoulders become rounded, our brown hair becomes white, our round faces become oval; but by the cunning artifice of memory, up come the features of the past--milestones of thirty years back, forty years back, fifty years back--unaltered.

They wear the same blue. They stand the same height. They are sheltered by the same green branches. They pass in and out of the same gate. They speak to us in the same tone of voice.

Thus it is as I look into the beautiful face before me. The veil of intervening years is lifted. I wander through the galleries of the past and again behold my mother in varying scenes--making the years which have swept by since she left me but as yesterday.

I see her in her remarkable ministry, holding spellbound great audiences distinguished for education and culture by her eloquent and faithful presentation of Gospel truths.

I see her by my father's side, with her exceptional intellectual resources disentangling knotty problems that confronted the movement in its early days.

I see her in heated controversy, her beautiful eyes aflame with spiritual understanding, as with logical and philosophical argument she confounds agnostic and unbeliever.

I see her in the light of the midnight lamp--her pen flying across the pages of every phase of life--writing upon the heart of generations yet to come through her imperishable books.

I see her standing in the doorway, while those who had come to her with faces shadowed with sorrow pass out with faces illumined with smiles.

But the memories most fascinating to me--upon which my mental vision lingers the fondest--are those which gather about her as "my mother."

I see her as she stands before the kitchen table mixing the wholewheat bread--which to be without, positively made our young hearts ache--her sweet face flushed by the heat from the old-fashioned range, and merry, as we told her no other fingers could make bread such as hers.

I see her laying aside her needlework (for my mother could fashion anything, from a hat to a shoe) to make our young hearts glad by mingling her laughter with our hilarity over the adventures of the day.

Lovely with an infinite preciousness is the picture of her giving to her children her evening blessing in prayer and song.

Then how inestimably sacred is memory's vision of her in her own room, in "mother's chair" by the window, renewing her spiritual vitality by the stream of living water that flows across the pages of the Bible!

But when through the illumined vistas of thought I am with her again in the closing hours of her sojourn here, I do not see the precious one fading from me in the damp dark mists of death. The chariot halts at her bedside, a light that is not from the rising or the setting of any earthly sun transforms her suffering features and she passes in through wide-swung gates to the Home of which she taught us.

On one of my late tours a gentleman expressed his views that there was no Heaven awaiting us in the Great Beyond. I replied, "You could never so persuade me to think, for I saw my mother pass in!"

It is not, therefore, to be wondered at that in the sorrows that have come to me, memory has brought her to my side, just as she always was, with her great heart of understanding sympathy, and made her, though absent in the flesh, my dearest and nearest consolation.

In temptation, her words of warning; in trial, her assurances of God's abundant grace; in fear, her strong entreaties never to depart from the highest and straightest path, have rung out as bells in my heart.

When in tumult of perplexity, pressed on every hand by difficulty, her shining example of where to seek and obtain wisdom has again and again marked a pathway out of the tangled maze. The memory of her loving deeds, her heroic sacrifices, her courageous and brilliant spirit, has been a beacon on the voyage of life, and she is with me today, this mother of mine, more precious, more living, because of the years between!

As I think upon her--her inestimable worth while she lived; her inestimable worth since she died--I feel there are no words to express how great a blessing is a Christian mother, or how great and choice a gift of God is this memory that brings into the midst of the struggle and weariness of later life the sweet, pure days and ways of our earliest years.

The only fair thing, and white thing, and tender thing in the lives of many, are these recollections which, like the snowy white foam of the cataract tumbling down the mountainside, come tumbling down the peaks of time, and we find ourselves after twenty, thirty, forty years, overwhelmed with memories.

They start up from the village, or the mill, or the wicket-gate, or the schoolhouse, or the old farm, or the Scotch hill, or the fisherman's boat. They carry us many years back. Our feet--a few sizes smaller--are traveling along the dust road of the town or hamlet we lived in. We stand again in the Sabbath-school and join in the hymns. We pass into the old schoolhouse. We sit on the bench our little legs dangled from and see again the sun strike slanting rays across the room, lighting up the well worn spotted desks, with their shabby inkwells, and showing clearly the white chalk marks on the blackboard. In those rays we see again the faces of the older pupils--scattered we know not where.

And, shining like a star of gold, we see mother! Mother, with her toils and her patience and her love and her prayers, and her dear sweet face and her soft silvery hair. Mother, who rocked our cradle. Mother, who mended our torn clothes. Mother, who sat by us when we were sick. Mother, who when we were wayward wept, and when we were repentant, forgave. Oh, my heart, how it throbs, how it yearns.

I can see her now--the shade of her dress, the shape of her little hand, the wondrous angel eyes--and hear again the tremor in the voice when she prayed, "Our dear loving Father, in Thy arms shield my children from sin and harm and at last gather them with Thy flock into Thy great fold in Heaven!"

"One lamp, thy mother's love, amid the stars shall lift its pure flame changeless, and before the throne of God burn throughout eternity."

My Father, the Founder

Excerpted from two articles in:
The War Cry (Chicago) April 9, 1932 and
The War Cry (Chicago) April 10, 1937.

How every one loved him! The whole world loved him. Surely never did the passing of any man in history call forth so great a tribute as surged around the cortege of my father, the Founder of The Salvation Army. From the nation's ruler, the city's pauper, the highest religious teacher, the poor condemned criminal, the university professor, the unlearned and untaught, the hospital's sick, the poor house's aged, crowned heads and presidents, the greatest philanthropists, commercial princes and the highest ecclesiastics of the Protestant, Catholic and Jewish faiths there came up a tide of love and appreciation such as history had never seen.

No scientist, or soldier, or philosopher, or statesman could be named among General Booth's contemporaries, whose name was honored in so many lands and whose passing caused such universal regret in every walk of human life.

Kings joined with peasants to lay wreaths upon his casket and, in almost every Parliament throughout the British Empire, resolutions were passed declarative of appreciation of his life's work and admiration for his personal character.

But nothing has been more striking to me than that so many of those who have both spoken and written in eulogistic terms of the General seemed to overlook the chief factor that made him great. They appear to have missed the primary cause of his marvelous influence over all mankind for good.

The forces which shaped his wonderful life lay in the spiritual realm. He used spiritual forces to serve spiritual ideals. Religion to him was not merely a sentiment, not merely a thing of the skies. It was a vibrating, abiding, deathless force. It was not of ascetic or monastic type. It trod the common earth. It took the form of a practical, instructed pity for every phase of human need. It asked that his love for God should find expression in his love for man. It was his religion that formed the foundation for his life's work, and he who builds by the forces which belong to religion builds higher and more enduringly than any one else.

Dr. Fitchett said, "If we agree to forget how religion may affect the next world, it is certain that nothing else so profoundly affects this world." "Religion," said Burke, "is the basis of civil society." And a French wit, in creed and temper the very antipode of Burke, said the same thing when he wrote, "If God did not exist it would be necessary to invent Him." "Religion is civilization, the very highest," said Disraeli. "The world would have committed suicide but for Christianity," said Mazzini. And George Washington embraced in his orders to the heroes of Valley Forge, "Let it be the highest ambition of every man to add to the distinguished character of patriot the much more gloriously distinguished character of Christian."

And the secret of my father's influencing the peoples of the world so powerfully for good was his Christianity, and his ability to apply his Christianity to all peoples was the secret of his unparalleled success.

It laid hold of dejected and fallen man by the hand and lifted him up. It rode in upon the highways of sin and misery and overcame wickedness with righteousness and supplanted sorrow with song. It lifted harbors of refuge from every storm that can beat against the body and beat against the soul.

It threw a protecting wing over defenseless childhood all around the globe. It erected homes of comfort for the aged and fulfilled the Scripture in making it "Light at eventide."

It put a song of cheer on the lips of the sailor at the masthead and carried consolation and help to the dying soldier on the gory fields of war. It made him to reach, to gather, to organize, direct and control by the strictest possible discipline a body of preachers and workers drawn from the masses and collected from all nations of the earth, such as the world has never seen.

But this was not the greatest. To infuse such a body with his own ardor, to give to it his own ideals, to impart unto it his own courage, to enkindle it with the fires of his own zeal, to make it to share voluntarily his own sacrifices, to stamp upon it his own piety and to do it on such an enormous scale, and to keep on doing it to the end of his lifetime--it is this that has been the factor upon which the whole world has wondered. For mighty as were his intellectual powers and magnetic as was his personality, it was not his human charms that drew us. It was his saintliness that attracted us, it was his divine courage that commanded us, it was his patience in suffering that lifted us, it was his charity toward his enemies that charmed us, it was his immovability in persecution that inspired us and it was his great heart, which was as a bottomless well, with its Christlike passion for the poor and lowly, that held us to his flag and to his God.

Sixty-seven years ago my father, returning home from that never to be forgotten visit to the East of London, declared to my beloved and ever-revered mother, "Kate, I have found my destiny."

What a destiny! To the uttermost poor, to the most hopelessly lost, to the forgotten and the neglected among men, to those who by the sheer vulgarity of their sins had made themselves social castaways, and, who, under the ever increasing weight of woe, were being thrust to the nethermost place in that world of the abandoned.

"Kate, I have found my destiny," and the intonation was not a dirge. It did not partake of the funereal. Unquestionably there was measureless pathos, but there was also boundless hope. The cry on that threshold was the offspring of a love that was not of earth. The import of that great sacrificial act sustained by the grace which begot it grows and grows with the passing years.

We see, much clearer than was possible sixty-seven years ago to our blessed Founder, the content and sweep of that word, "destiny." Then it was limited to a group and a neighborhood that called for sacrificial toil because of the extremity of the need. A world movement never entered the wildest imagination. But there was upon that London thoroughfare released a force that has made an ever growing impact upon the life of the whole world and today, as a result of that discovery and that devotion we have The Salvation Army.

To study this movement is to study the man who made it. The Founder is known by his product. As the years roll by I am persuaded that the world is getting nearer to a correct appraisal of the life of my revered father, whose toil brought The Salvation Army.

This marvelous movement is an abiding and an ever growing, because ever living, testimony to the probity of the man who gave it to the world.

Although he went from us long since, he will forever live most vigorously and most beneficently. He lives in thousands of ministering agencies, which he created and set in motion the world over. These all have the power of reproducing themselves, so that in that "destiny" my father discovered in the haunts of the dejected poor, there was, though unseen, fabulous wealth for the enrichment of the race. This has written the name of William Booth in ineffaceable lettering upon every sky and has enshrined forever his memory in the heart of the world.

The greatest legacy the Founder left us is the spirit of his life.

To preserve this is our chief task. The wonderful mechanism of The Salvation Army would cease to function effectively if ever shorn of that spirit. The vision of my father is ever before me. Crowning all his splendid, and in many aspects his unique, human abilities was the imparted spirit of his Master, to whom he ever ascribed all glory for the inestimable good that flowed through his life in the revelation of that "destiny," to which Heavenly vision he was ever obedient.

It was this spirit which made the hearts of his great audience receive without resentment the most cutting utterances in denouncement of sin man ever uttered from public places. It was this spirit, this conviction of "his destiny" that bore him triumphant over innumerable tides of bitter opposition. It was this spirit which when he was honored by the greatest of all lands, chained his thoughts, his toils, his life's greatest passion to the common people.

The same path and the same all qualifying Lord are available to us each, and Founder's Day will be the most blessedly commemorated as we each address ourselves in God's name and by God's power to the task of preserving and amplifying this gloriously rich gift my father left us.

A Personal Memory

The last time I was with him he had an address to deliver in Albert Hall, in London. He was 83 years old, and stood six feet one. Those grey, eagle eyes were unseeing, but they ranged from pit to gallery as if his will would force them to report to his brain. Clasped behind his straight back were his hands, lovely things molded so beautifully that sculptors hungered to copy them. The lights of the hall found a sheen in his white hair and beard, and I tried to watch that and forget his poor eyes.

"I am going into dry dock for repairs," he told them.

We came home from Albert Hall and had some tea. He never took sugar. In fact, he had lived so abstemiously that his body was then less frail than it had been in his youth. He had perfect control of his appetites.

"Let me wait until after the operation," I begged.

"No, Eva. I am going to see better than in a score of years. You go back to your work in America."

He was in his dressing gown, on his knees, praying at his bed, when I dropped down beside him and he snuggled me against him.

Something went wrong in the operation. An infection developed, and so he came to the end of his days in utter darkness. He wrote me a letter of farewell, forming his letters from memory. I've got that little bit of scribble now.

"I've done my best for God with my eyes," he wrote. "Now I'll do it without eyes."

They tried to get him to take more nourishment. There was a strike in East London at the time.

"Poor women can't get milk to feed their babies," he railed, "and you bring me eggs!" Soon after that he died.

Chapter Three
The Booth Family

Gone Home (Herbert Booth)

Evangeline Booth's tribute to her brother, Herbert, at his funeral. Privately published (no date) by his widow, Annie W. Booth. Herbert was promoted to Glory on September 25, 1926.

There is a better world than this. We are born for a higher destiny than earth. We believe it. We teach it. We preach it. And yet we forget it. We become absorbed in earthly interests; absorbed in our occupations; in our trials and conflicts and difficulties. So absorbed in our ministry for the good of mankind as to forget its heavenly termination. And there is a knock at our doors; or a hand is laid upon the heart of one beloved; or the ringing call of a bugle from distant hills. It is the announcement of the chariot halting at our gate, and then we all freshly realize there is a Home eternal in the heavens because the light in the eyes of our loved ones as they bid us farewell tells us so.

My dear brother, Herbert Booth, was endowed with exceptional gifts. Like our beloved father, the Founder of The Salvation Army, he had the genius for organization.

He possessed those qualities so necessary to all leaders of men--the qualities of creating conditions and circumstances which served the purposes he had at heart.

He was a natural pioneer. He never lacked the courage required for initiative work; never shrank from shouldering the responsibility resulting from his own judgment, decisions and deeds. He was fearless when face to face with an opponent, dauntless in persecution and adversity, brave in the storm did the winds come down from the high places or come up from the low. True at every cost, every time and everywhere, from the beginning to the end, to his convictions and his teaching.

These characteristics made him of the greatest value to our father (the Founder of the worldwide Salvation Army) in its early years--indeed, he was responsible for many of the aggressive features of our organization, and the Founder entrusted him with such large commands as Great Britain, Canada and Australia.

He was a preacher of exceptional ability. Oh, how he gloried in the Gospel! He believed that it was effective and sufficient whenever and wherever applied; and, like his glorified father and his earlier mentor, he was constantly crying, "Woe is me if I preach not the Gospel!" And he preached it--all of it--the full Gospel, and God wonderfully honored him.

But perhaps the gift which was the most strikingly distinctive was that of a composer. His compositions in the Gospel hymns and for brass bands, have gone round the world, attracting and winning thousands of souls for the Kingdom of God.

For years he rendered a greater service to the Army than anyone else connected with the organization in the direction of music and song, and this talent, coupled with his passion for music, associated his name with the brass bands and songs of The Salvation Army in a way that can never be separated.

Those songs enrich lastingly the hymnology of The Salvation Army and the whole Church of God. As they lowered my precious mother into her grave the vast surrounding crowd sang:

"Blessed Lord, in Thee is refuge,
  Safety for my trembling soul,
Power to lift my head when drooping,
  'Midst the angry billows roll;
  I will trust Thee,
All my life Thou shalt control."

That song he gave to us in life, and he now bequeaths it to us in death.

Who can say what soul-help has flowed and is flowing and will flow from that gem:

"Grace there is my every debt to pay,
Blood to wash my every sin away,
Power to keep me spotless day by day"

to the multitudes who have and do and will sing such hope-inspiring, strength-imparting words?

"Yet shall he live" in the sweet cadency and rhythmical flow of his glorious music and in the lilting strength and depth of those stanzas that voice the heart-longings of those oppressed with sin and sorrow and the searchers after God.

The musicians here today, therefore, represent tens of thousands of Salvation Army bandsmen the world over who are lovingly grateful for this consecrated gift of my brother's.

It is impossible to make a comprehensive survey of his life on an occasion such as this. His affection as a relative, his devotion as a friend, his grace as a Christian, his patience as a sufferer, his vision as a poet, his eloquence as a preacher, his power as a composer, his fidelity and his forceful effectiveness as an evangelist all call for enlarged comment, quite impossible within the limits of the hour, so I must reserve it all for a future effort.

When the time came for my brother to separate himself from the Army, when he felt called to an independent work, the Lord continued to abundantly bless his evangelistic efforts, and though removed from under our Flag he persevered in his warfare upon the great battlefields of righteousness and truth. And so we still fought unitedly under the banner of Calvary.

But above and beyond all the lights of his gifts and even service shone the lamp of his Christian character.

The more one came to know him personally the more convinced was one that his eyes were fastened on his Lord and Savior, ever seeking to find His footsteps, that he might shine forth in His likeness. His spirit was sweet. His manner gentle. His heart was loving and very quick to forgive. He kept his soul in unbroken communion with his Savior.

To me he was very dear. It is not always found that the ties of blood are enriched by the quality of understanding or that therein the bond of friendship lives. Oftentimes brothers fail in adverse circumstances, but not so with my brother Herbert. He was always available, and his counsel and guidance were always wise and exalting. I am here to testify that in him there lived that additional quality of the "Friend that sticketh closer than a brother." Beautiful as were the ties of kinship, causing gladness of heart, it is still a greater joy to me to witness at Herbert's funeral that he added to these the strong and inspiring characteristic of a loyal and devoted friend.

He was a true brother, and since he came to reside here at Yonkers we have had many times of sweet communion and helpfulness together.

We never met, either in my home or I in his, but we prayed side by side to the God of our father and mother, and the comfort of his tender affection and support of his goodwill toward me and my work I shall keenly miss.

It is most natural that I, his bereaved and sorrowing sister, should find comfort in reflection upon the words of an all-sympathetic and all-understanding Friend who once entered the home of bereft sisters and said, "Thy brother shall rise again." Similarly He comes to me with the same all-heartening truth and, while I sorrow, it is not for a moment as do those without hope. Dissolution claims our loved one, for the tabernacle was but earthly, but the building to which he, by grace, has winged his flight is enduring--"eternal in the heavens." The storm has shattered the dwelling terrestrial, but no hurricane will ever mar or touch the mansion celestial.

All our hearts go out to dear Mrs. Booth, whose loss will be inestimable--her love and devotion to him were unbounded--and to his devoted Christian son Henry, his dear wife and four little children.

We must pray that the great Healer of all wounds and Consoler of all sorrows will dry their tears.

While we know that saving grace does not descend from the father to the children, yet blessings do come to the children and the children's children, and my brother has so lived that his children shall rise up to call him blessed.

Then we must remember we shall all meet at Home.

When our father was in Chicago last he was very ill and quite a little delirious. Sitting by his side in the early hours of one morning, his mind wandered back to the years when we were children and used to be taken out for our daily walk.

My father mistook me for my mother and, laying his fevered fingers upon my hand, said my mother's name. "Kate, Kate, don't worry, don't be anxious. It is dusk, I know, but all the children will be safe, they will all come home in good time." And then he repeated the name of each member of the family again, saying, "They will all come home in good time."

My brother, as he passed away, opened his eyes very wide and fixed them very high.

Through the dusk of the passing I could see expression of recognition in them and whispered to Mrs. Booth to ask him if he was going home to our mother.

Before she could repeat the words he nodded his head twice.

Then I said, "Herbert, dear, if there is a light in the valley, and if you realize that the Great Shepherd is with you as you pass through the shadows, try and lift your hand that our hearts may be comforted." He threw up his two arms above his head and fixed his eyes very, very high.

I knew well his vision clearly saw that which our mortal eyesight could not catch, and I thought upon the words:

"Then I shall see Him face to face,
And tell the story--saved by grace"

as out of the dusk he passed into his eternal Home. Perfect purity, fullness of joy, everlasting freedom, sweetest rest and eternal reunion.

"His servants serve Him and see His face."

My Sister's Sorrow (Emma Booth-Tucker)

Evangeline Booth-Tucker, infant daughter of the American co-commander, died at the age of three months. Commissioner Evangeline hurried from Toronto to New York to comfort her sister and to conduct the funeral service. Her tiny namesake is buried in Kensico Cemetery, near the Consul and baby William, who also died in infancy.

From The War Cry (Toronto) October 15, 1898

While my soul was yet palpitating in sympathy with the bitter heartthrobs of my bereaved comrade Mrs. Read, a sudden summons called me to where, 'neath the lowering of dark sorrow's wing, some bound to me by tenderest ties of love and war were gathered. Ere I reached the home of our American leaders the threatening weight of affliction had fallen and the little life lent for those few all too short months had taken its flight to the eternal sunshine. As I looked upon the transparent features of my sister's baby daughter who was also my namesake, I could not help feeling that they were too fair to do battle with this world's storms and sin, and was not surprised to hear that even when the baby appeared the healthiest, as well as the most beautiful of children, the Commander had termed her "a little breath from Heaven."

With rare intelligence in one so young the baby had already given evidence of a tender and sympathetic nature which, had it been the will of God to mature, would have doubtless brought infinite blessing and balm in the holy warfare to which the little one had been dedicated. "You could not cry in her presence," says one who watched her, and when, at some painful verdict of the doctor, drops of grief fell upon the fragile little form, the big blue eyes would fill and the tiny face upon which the light of a heavenly world already rested seemed to reflect the sorrow written upon the agony of mother love which bent over her.

Of the intensity of grief which has borne down the brave spirit of my darling sister the Consul, I feel it is impossible to speak. She has suffered and sorrowed with all the depth of her acutely sensitive heart. The physical strain of the three weeks of unremittent watching and anxiety has made very heavy inroads upon her slender store of strength, and I am asking that the prayers of the Canadian Territory should unite with the petitions of those across the border to the God of all sufficiency and strength, that His tenderest support may be given to the Consul in this trying hour.

It was my painful privilege to lay the little one to rest, and in the pathos of that baby's funeral I learnt something of the heavenly influences which that tiny messenger from the spirit world had wielded upon so great a number of hearts in that city of New York.

The child-spirit stands with her little cousin, my darling sister Lucy's little Evangeline, in the beauty of eternal day--my two little representatives before the Throne--creating, by her transplanting to the skies, another link binding me to the Eternal Homeland.

Bramwell Booth

A. My Brother - An Appreciation

Upon his succession to the Generalship. From The War Cry (New York) December 28, 1912.

Perhaps no man has had more synonyms found for his name, more analogies for his character, than has my brother.

In him some have seen Joshua, who took up the work when the great lawgiver was gathered to his fathers and led Israel's wandering feet into the Promised Land; while others have declared him Elisha, upon whom fell the mantle of miraculous power when the Prophet of Fire was hurried by lambent steeds into the glory of his reward.

Flanking these illustrations, there have been brought up battalions of names famous in the history of war, Church and State. Many men have seen in him many heroes, but a composite photograph of their encomiums would reveal the picture of one in gifts of great versatility, of strong, winning personality and deeply genuine spirituality.

So the world sums up the figure which above all others now stands out in the Army's foreground. But it is not as in the mirror of simile I would speak of him here, but rather allow some actual aspects of his individuality to acclaim the man.

As a Writer

Although he has found time amid his multifarious duties to pay flying visits to our comrades on the Continent of Europe, the real day of his travels is to come; and thus to the majority of the Army world the fiery eloquence of public utterances is still unheard. Yet his teachings are already household words among us all, for one of his best and most effective weapons is the all-powerful pen. The General is essentially a man of letters. Originality of thought, and the aptitude for framing it, are alike instinctive with him. His books stand foremost in the literary treasures of our organization and, backed as are their pages with a passionate love for the souls of men, their message cuts through and beyond the mind and grips the very soul. Prose has chiefly claimed his pen, yet there have been some poems which have immortalized themselves upon the conscience of the community. Only in that day when the secret struggles and unsung victories of the life of the soul are disclosed shall we know the fullness of the cup of blessing carried to tens of thousands of parched spirits in the verse:

"Oh, when shall my soul find her rest,
  My strugglings and wrestlings be o'er?
My heart, by my Savior possessed,
  Be fearing and sinning no more."

or its inspired companion:

"Now search me, and try me, O Lord!
Now, Jesus, give ear to my cry!
See, helpless I cling to Thy word,
My soul to my Savior draws nigh."

As a Worker

If doctors were infallible, then our present General ought to have been dead long ago, for they have passed again and again the severest condemnations upon the pace he has kept up for years. Despite a physique which, though commanding in appearance, is far from being constitutionally robust; despite a diet which is almost scanty and always strictly abstemious; despite a burden of responsibility weighty enough to break the back of a Hercules, his ordinary day's work, from the time he took his place at my father's right hand, has been that of several ordinary men. His labors sometimes start soon after dawn and end only when the next is approaching, for it is not exceptional for the General to climax a long and hard day by conducting a half-night of prayer, to which he comes up with a freshness and vim which make his astonished staff feel like reechoing the comment made by the Swedish soldier upon his royal idol, Gustavus Adolphus, "The king is best at the close of the day."

As an Administrator

It is a difficult proposition to attempt to estimate the number, much more to specify the important character, of the reins which have been held in these strong hands for years.

The peculiarities, possibilities, perils, positions and powers of all peoples of the earth are but a small quota of the subjects momentarily retained upon the mental retina of his vision.

But he is a born statesman, with the ability to turn from the abstract to the concrete at a moment's notice, and at the mastery of detail he is a marvel. The officer interviewed upon the opening of operations in a great heathen empire does not find him more interested and informed than the comrade dealt with regarding an obscure and seemingly unimportant factor in a social institution.

The General's administration is invariably characterized by four traits-- intuition, caution, skill and courage.

I say intuition. The enemy has not to travel to his door to make him conscious of the many roads over which he could pass. And so he has all his gates closed, and every protective fortress lifted, in case of necessity; hence, a multitude of times, when other leaders would have found themselves overtaken, the General's marvelous intuition has triumphed.

I say caution, because with the infinite pains which are the hallmark of genius, he refuses to sacrifice safety to speed, and insists upon the presentation of every side of a case before deciding upon it.

I say skill, because perhaps there is no man living who has had so to manipulate the warp and woof of the thread of life--a momentous task and dangerous in less wise, less conscientious and less consecrated hands.

I say courage. Courage is an indispensable quality to a leader of men; this has been a conspicuous characteristic of my brother. Not only capable of strong, deeply rooted convictions, but never lacking in dauntless courage to execute those convictions, despite the bitterest opposition or the heaviest cost. In the tempestuous storms which have beaten upon our great vessel in its rough voyage in the form of disaster, or threats of planned destruction and hurt which have come to us from our enemies, then this fearless and admirable soldier quality has made him our Napoleon.

As a Son

In this relationship he was wonderful as well as beautiful. As the son of the great founder of our Movement, his character has glowed in its most brilliant light--not, perhaps, out before the world, but before his God and those closest to him in his position, chiefly behind the scenes.

From a youth, his understanding sympathy in all disappointments; his quickness to grasp the particular features which constituted trying conditions; his utter oblivion to self-gain, or physical claims, or personal notoriety, when aid, small or momentous, could be rendered his father and General, made him a pillar of strength in council, an unsurpassed comfort in sorrow, a veritable Rock of Gibraltar in emergency, that far outreached what is generally understood by the right-hand man or a faithful armor bearer.

The unbroken forty years of nervous strain and hidden toils which have come within the limit of this devotion have prematurely whitened his hair; but the silver only lends a remarkable setting to the great dark eyes, which reveal a remarkable soul, as they look out from a remarkable face into the depth of your heart.

My brother comes into the Generalship with a wealth of love at his feet because of what he proved himself to be through the long years he stood at the side of his father.

A gentleman, speaking of my father, quoted the words of Harriet Martineaux, "Whenever I saw him I thought of what the first man must have been--God's ideal man." And so I think of the General of today--my brother!

B. What America Thinks of the General

Upon his first visit to the United States. From The War Cry (New York) March 4, 1916.

Outspoken speech has been set down as both America's greatest virtue and its greatest fault. Whatever the opinion of reader or writer, it is certain that no one who steps into public view, be he visitor or resident, is left long in doubt as to the country's feeling toward him. When it is one of distrust there are usually more or less discomfiting evidences, and when it is one of confidence there is equally abundant demonstration, for, far from being abashed,

America takes some pride in "wearing its heart upon its sleeve."

When the visit of the General to this country--that long looked for event--transpired, there was a rush of expressions telling that the American public in general and The Salvation Army in particular, had taken its illustrious guest into its heart, after the wholesale, enthusiastic fashion of the nation. During the more than two years which have elapsed since those remarkable weeks there have come to me, both directly and indirectly, the feelings and thoughts which the General called forth and, while the following are by no means the sum and total, they are at least the most salient of such sentiments:

1. He looks the part. Perhaps some communities might be inclined to discredit this consideration as unworthy of weight, but there is no gainsaying the fact that in America appearances do count for something. Not necessarily symmetry of line or perfection of physique, but dignity, demeanor--in short, an impressive appearance often wins the first hearing. Hence there were those who confessed to an almost breathless curiosity to look for the first time upon the face of the new General. The patriarchal figure of the Army's Founder had photographed itself indelibly upon the mental retina of the nation, and it was commonly felt and said that every line of his face and form bespoke the great character of the man as well as the magnitude of his work. This being so,

the keen anxiety which prevailed to behold the personality of his successor was only natural. It was a thrilling moment when the great crowd of Salvationists awaiting the General's arrival at the Grand Central Station heaved a sigh of relief as the noted figure stepped before them. On first appearances he had not disappointed them. "I like your looks," were his trenchant, opening words and, as though commissioned to voice the unanimous response of the mighty throng gathered there, a man's stentorian tones rang through the world's greatest concourse and echoed across its artificial, star-studded sky, "We like yours, General!"

Here are some of the characteristics of his appearance which captivated them:

a. The General's height. This alone was a tremendous bid for favor. America likes big men. As some one facetiously observes, "It likes its Davids to be Goliaths." With but few exceptions, the nation's heroes have been and are men of many inches. Therefore we understand the rather colloquially expressed feelings of one who remarked, "You bet, there's plenty of him, and it's all General!"

b. His military bearing. It is not alone the gold crest or field marshal's cape--it is the way these are worn that makes the shoulders instinctively straighten and the hand instinctively lift to the salute.

c. His remarkable face. "The eye of a dreamer and the mouth of a master of men," was one comment. "In every speaking feature one can trace a brilliant destiny," was another. "I looked into his face and saw the great man behind the great rank," was a third.

2. His intensity compels men. I question whether halfheartedness or indifference ever "gets anywhere" in any land, but I am quite sure that in America the man who makes his mark and leaves it upon others is he who lives and breathes and radiates his purpose. The General is tremendously in earnest about the vitalities of Salvationism. "They mean everything to me--they must mean everything to you"--that is the impression he left in the metropolis of the New World. The General makes an audience feel that the revelations of God concerning righteousness and sin are his meat and drink--his very existence--and it makes no difference whether an audience numbers a thousand or one.

3. His liberality of vision attracts men. Side by side and quite harmoniously with his rooted adherence to the Articles of our Faith and

Regulation, there is growing a large heart's tolerance for the peculiarities, nay more, the frailties of others. Some of the sacred expressions which proclaimed his liberality of vision in the officers' councils have graven themselves as memorials on the grateful recollection of his people. His ability to grasp, and patience with, the limitations of the human, coupled with the tenacity with which he unfalteringly holds to the limitless ability of the Divine, attracted unanimous admiration and trust.

4. His simplicity wins men. He is too great to be grand. His addresses are talks composed of small syllables dipped in fire. He makes little use of either complicated language or philosophical thought--his themes are too immense to require it. Jesus Christ stands to him in the stead of all. The name of Christ, which is always in his mouth; the mysteries of the Gospel, which he so divinely announces, make him omnipotent in his simplicity. When before the people his utterances are like sparks struck out, and wherever they fall they burn.

But it was not only the simplicity of the General's language which was so attractive over here, it was the simplicity of his whole demeanor, the utter absence of anything affected, which won the admiration and affection of all classes.

Lastly, America thinks that the General is the man for the present world's tragedy. There may be difference of opinion as to whether various political leaders are the men for the present emergency, but every American Salvationist, and many outside our ranks, are agreed that the General of The Salvation Army is the man for the hour. In this momentous upheaval of the nations our soul is turned upon the unpretentious room on International Headquarters which is the brain and heart-center of The Salvation Army. We see there a man weighed down with a big and growing realization of the tremendous issues at stake, their frightful cost in blood and tears and their varying effects upon the wide-flung battalions over which he rules; we feel his inflexible determination to keep first the two great governing principles of all Christianity--love for God and love for our fellow men; to lose not sight of the Salvationist's goal, to live his creed in deeds of mercy and lives of purity before all distracted peoples. We pin our faith in these stormy times to the heart of the man upon whose shoulders and spirit the mantle of our great Founder has fallen, and believe that he shall lead the way before the nations, and the people of the four winds shall follow him and be gathered into the fold of the blessed.

With Love to Marian

Evangeline often revealed her tender affection for her invalid sister, Staff-Captain Marian B. Booth (better known as "Marie"), who "endured patiently and fruitfully years of weakness and ill health." The following is a personal letter from Evangeline to Marian, June 4, 1934.

PERSONAL
E.C.B.

Staff-Captain Marie Booth
Cumberland Court
484 Seven Sisters Road
Finsbury Park
London, N. 4, England

My precious, precious Sister Marie:

I wish it were possible to let you know how continually you are in my thoughts, how constantly my heart sends up a prayer to our Heavenly Father, our mother and our father's God, and how often your dear face comes before me as it was when I saw you last.

Dear Marie, I am more happy than I can say that I am coming over to see you. It will be wonderful for you and me and dear Lucy to be together again. I am so pleased that Lucy has been taking such good care of you and that you are so happily and comfortably fixed up in a nice little apartment.

Now I want Lucy to write me and tell me of anything you want in the way of clothes. I think I can bring it from America a little nicer and "smarter" than we could get it over there, also with less expense as the pound has gone up so much in England.

Anyway you must think of something that it would be nice for you to have and let me know in time to get it made and bring it with me. But I am writing a line to Lucy on the subject by this same mail, so you need not give it a single thought except to say just what you would most like to have.

Yours in tenderest affection

A Message from the General in India

Excerpts from Evangeline's tribute at the funeral of Staff-Captain Marian B. Booth; who was promoted to Glory on January 6, 1937 at the age of 72.

"When she prayed, I always felt that the distance between earth and Heaven was shortened. Her appeals quickly reached the Throne of Grace.

"Song brought her great joy. In the night hours, her devoted Nurse Craven told me, her voice would ring out with some beautiful chorus. Throughout my Campaign in India, the echoes of her last song and prayer have been with me.

"It is a great comfort that my sister, Commissioner Lucy, who has nursed her for the past three years, will be at the service to speak for her.

"We must go straight on, growing gentler, stronger, truer, leaving upon the ways we tread the impress of a broad, sweet charity."

Beloved Consul

A published letter from Commissioner Evangeline to her sister, Consul Emma Booth-Tucker, when the Booth-Tuckers succeeded her in her first (temporary) American command. Note: Evangeline had guided the American forces through an extremely difficult time in the Army's history. From The War Cry (New York) April 11, 1896.

Beloved Consul: On behalf of the National Headquarters and the whole of the American field, to whom I have had the pleasure of holding the relationship of temporary Commissioner for a brief period, I write to convey to you sympathy and greeting.

The record of your past career as a leader of the Lord's hosts has preceded you to this country. My American comrades have listened to and have been thrilled by many touching stories relating to the care and sympathy exhibited towards those successful officers on the United States field who were trained under your personal supervision. Characters innumerable have been widened and deepened, spirits inspired and set on flame of the Holy Ghost and hearts melted and touched with Calvary-love through your ministrations, and today, in common with every other country in which the Blood-and-Fire Flag is unfolded to the breeze, the United States field is richly endowed with a consecrated woman leadership, a percentage of which date their success from the moment they received your welcome from the International Training Home steps, and delight to address you with that most endearing of all appellations, "Mother."

American comrades have learned to love you, also, for the brightness you have brought into thousands of hearts and lives through your public meetings, and for the brave and uncompromising manner in which you have unfurled the standard of holiness and drawn around it a multitude of those struggling in the darkness of doubt and sin.

They love you for the sacrifice you have made, at the General's call, to leave all and come over to lead forward our Army forces, despite the awful calamity which has so recently overtaken them. What that sacrifice has meant to you none but God and yourself can ever know. As we ponder the same, visions float before us of a tender parting, with a loved babe which has since been carried by an angel to Heaven. My precious sister, brave hearts beat beneath Salvation uniforms on American soil, but tears are no disgrace to the bravest of us, and American comrades mingle, in spirit, tears with those of their loved new leaders in this the day of your sorrow, and pray God comfort you!

Last, but far from least, the troops here welcome you for the sterling service they have known you to render the General by your valued counsel during years gone by, and can somewhat appreciate the sacrifice he has made for the interests of America in parting with you.

America none the less welcomes the well and tried leader, your husband, Commander Booth-Tucker. What we know of him tells us that he is winging his way to this land with mind and heart full of plans and schemes of a glorious character, to pour out with Niagara force upon this country for its salvation.

Although being in command here for so short a time, the exceptionable storm of the hour has given me so intimate knowledge of the American troops that I can say with all confidence that you step to lead forth a people who will joyfully rally around you, hold up your hands in battle, strengthen your heart with prayer, follow you closely beneath the Blood-and-Fire Flag; a people that, having done all, will be found standing fast in the faith, true to their God, true to your leadership and true to the principles of the worldwide Salvation Army.

For myself, I think they are a precious people, and have learned dearly to love them, while I look upon their new Commanders as among the dearest and most valued of all leaders.

Chapter Four

Salvation Army Personalities

Lt. Commissioner Richard Griffith

A tribute to her loyal secretary for more than four decades, who died suddenly on the platform just prior to one of her meetings. From the Library of the School for Officers' Training, Suffern, N.Y. No date given or information as to its publication.

The sudden parting with Lt. Commissioner Griffith, my armor bearer of over forty years, brave and selfless, has thrown around me the shadow of a great sorrow. How extraordinary is that sorrow only those who were intimately acquainted with his life can possibly know. The manner in which he gave himself in an unmeasured and lifetime devotion to one single purpose, associated with my life given to the same purpose, can seldom have been paralleled.

Never can I forget the tumult of thought and feeling which surged through my being when I was told that he had gone--gone from his place by my side; gone in the midst of his labors; gone in the full vigor of his life; gone--as the lightning flashes--in a single second that left no time for a parting word or even for his customary expression when a difficult task had been completed, "There, that's finished and done!"

Better for him that he has gone up the Shining Road; and the manner of his going was that of instantaneous translation, without pain, without even a quick breath. But to the Army, and especially to me who received his incalculable support in prominent leadership through more than forty laborious years across many lands and many seas, his removal is a mysterious visitation.

As a young man Richard Griffith was confronted with many opportunities to make a career, to any one of which he would have brought powers that gave sure promise of success. From them all he turned away. Against them all he closed his mind. Except one. That one opportunity, with divine discernment of soul, he recognized in The Salvation Army. In his single and undeviating devotion to the high purpose which then flashed upon his vision, in his refusal to admit even the approach of any lesser inducement and in his ability to magnify the smallest duty by making it serve this one great purpose of his life, he has left for officers, no matter of what branch of Army service, an example which will ever shine with a lustre that is not of this world.

From the time when Commissioner Griffith, as a youth of twenty, first came to my side I ever found him to be a true Salvationist. He never knew anything, and never wanted to know anything, but the Army. When but a little boy of six or seven and on into his teens, he suffered many privations, traveling with his father through Wales and Canada and playing the cello when so small that he had to stand to accomplish the task. Yet his saintly father and mother told me they had never heard him complain.

The Salvation Army filled all his past and all his future. To its cause he surrendered his utmost of mind and energy as well as his tender, compassionate heart, and he ofttimes expressed deep regret that he had no more to give. He dwelt in God because he dwelt in love, and demonstrated in his life that we can do more good by being good than in any other way. He was a man of exceptional ability along many lines. His breadth of mind gave to him a wisdom that made his judgment of great worth, and this, coupled with his refinement of nature and nobility of character, rendered him especially fitted for his important confidential position.

Ungrudgingly he laid his life on the altar of Christ's service, and in a measure that I have known in but few he spent himself in the performance of duties that were endless and arduous. It seemed as if he were never a moment still, and many were aware--as I who knew him best could not fail to be aware--that he did not cease to spend and be spent until that last grand but awful moment when he went to be with his Lord.

Not less than for his industry and his Christlike devotion I valued the Commissioner for his unfaltering loyalty. He was loyal to everyone. Not once did he betray a confidence. He was a great friend. He knew the pure, unadulterated meaning of friendship, because friendship was a virtue that had been planted by God in his nature. And this allied with his selfless soul made him a willing and close follower of any one to whom his service was pledged. Yet in his sweet, happy contentment to follow he was in reality leading the way.

On land and sea, abroad as well as at home, in the throes of stormy circumstance as also in times of calm and easy progress, on the public platform and in the obscurity of the office, he was equally to be relied on, thus meeting the supreme demand of a secretary.

Seeking no praise, asking no gratitude, avoiding any prominence, he found his abundant reward in the knowledge that he had served.

At Bristol, on the day that the Commissioner was taken, he was eager in explaining to me the spiritual influence of the bandsmen and singers who took part in the Congress Festival the night before. Especially was he taken with the comrade who played the dulcimer and sang, exclaiming, "Oh, the spirit with which he did sing!"

Returning to the hotel from the festival the Commissioner was earnestly engaged until half-past one o'clock on Sunday morning dealing with a businessman about his soul. Though I was obliged to call him early to attend to some writing he never mentioned the matter to me--I learned of it afterward from another. Indeed it has seemed to me that in his service he was like Michelangelo, who carried a candle in his pasteboard cap so as not to throw his shadow upon any work in which he was engaged.

One of Commissioner Griffith's chief concerns was that he spare me pain. This arose out of his own gentle disposition. From a child I have been acutely alive to the sufferings of others. The passing of time and the hardness of the battle have not lessened this sensitiveness. Through the long years the Commissioner was noble and gracious in protecting me, as far as lay in his power, from pain and shock of any kind, and when the bad news had to come he was ever near and ever strove to soften the blow.

Messages which have reached me from many parts of the world have intensified my sense of immeasurable loss because of their glowing confirmation of the Commissioner's worth upon the wide battlefields whereon he stood with me. I am moved to profound gratitude for the blessing of his example upon Army comrades of all ranks, as well as upon those in varied stations outside the borders of the Army with whom he made contact in the course of our worldwide travels and my executive work. He reformed others unconsciously by his unbroken and unfaltering walk upward.

To come into contact with Commissioner Griffith was to respect and love him. I know of no one who did not do so. There was a sweetness about him which, down whatever pathway he passed, created goodwill. I think it was that sweetness which comes with the eagerness to serve anybody and all-- the little child, youth or old age. It was the opportunity to bless and cheer that fascinated him. Yet while he pitied the sinner there was no lack of condemnation of sin. An act of meanness or treachery toward another brought his spirit to red heat.

While I shall miss the wisdom of his sound judgment, his almost phenomenal patience in conflict, in storm and irritation, I think that which I shall miss the most will be his fine ability to discover and bring to my notice the bright spot in disadvantageous circumstances and the good in those who had erred and missed the way. All this he was by faith in the saving Gospel of Jesus Christ, the Sacrifice of the Lamb of God on the Cross.

Oh, my dear officers! As I write, my desires reach out to God not only for myself, but for you who are vastly dearer to me than myself. Let us pray for a greater trust in His power, His love, His mercy, His compassion beyond comprehension.

From the quick step of the Commissioner's departure may there be given to us a glimpse of the glory that awaits His children. May those whose eyes have tears see a new light, and if there be one who in any sense has wandered, may that one see the road back, wide and open. May our disappointments give to us tender blessings, and our sorrows healing for any sore places in our hearts.

Evangeline Booth
General

He Stands Out a Figure Alone: Samuel Logan Brengle

The subheading for this article reads:

"An eloquent and masterly address of eulogy and appreciation of the work of Commissioner Brengle on his official retirement from active service."

From The War Cry (New York) October 17, 1931.

Commissioner Brengle's gifts are so well known that there is nothing I can say about him with which you are not already familiar.

He has written his name across the hearts of the rank and file of The Salvation Army world, and what he is, and what God has enabled him to accomplish cannot be added to by the words of anyone.

The Commissioner has lived his life and performed his service with an eye so single to the glory of God that either the praise or the blame of any man is of little worth to him.

He looks with loving confidence to the "well done" from a Higher Source.

Yet it is fitting that I should make appropriate references to so worthy and conspicuous a warrior upon the occasion of his retirement.

The particular quality of Commissioner Brengle's gifts, the advanced nature of his education, the beauty of his character and his spiritual experience have peculiarly singled him out in the long line of Salvation Army officers, from the highest to the lowest ranks.

While closely allied to all of us by a thousand bonds, he stands out a figure alone!

He stands out because he has stood. He has stood for every purpose embraced in his calling. Stood a veritable Rock of Gibraltar for all the fundamentals inseparably associated with the soldier and with the saint.

In looking for a text upon which to base my remarks tonight upon this remarkable warrior of ours my eye fell upon these words, "And behold a certain lawyer stood up..."

The STAND-UP psychology has always appealed to me.

This standing up for righteousness and truth, portrayed in Christian heroes, has fascinated me from my earliest years. I have been thrilled as I read of Paul's standing before King Agrippa and Elijah standing before Ahab and fearlessly delivering God's message.

John Knox stood up before Queen Mary, denouncing her for her policies, until the tears flowed down her guilty cheeks. Martin Luther stood up before the Diet of Worms. John Bright, at the time of the Crimean War, stood up in the British Parliament and, in one of the greatest perorations that ever fell upon the human ear, said, "It is all very well for you to talk war, but hear the angels of death beating their wings over every home in the land." William Booth stood up and called for a people to stand up!

No greater mistake could a soldier make than to think he can drive back the enemies of the bodies and souls of men sitting down. Stand up!

COMMISSIONER BRENGLE HAS STOOD UP!

HE HAS STOOD UP FOR THE GOSPEL OF JESUS CHRIST--an unadulterated Gospel; a whole Gospel; the Gospel the Bible proclaims and the Army teaches, which he believes and lives; the Gospel with its solemn judgments; the Gospel with its saving grace from all depths to all heights; the Gospel with its stern line of demarcation between the right and the wrong; the Gospel with its fullness of love; the Gospel with its unlimited power; the Gospel with the great price in Blood paid to secure it its authority and its efficacy.

Commissioner Brengle has stood for this when difficult to do so and when easy. He has stood for this in private and in public. He has stood for this with those dear to him and with those opposed to him.

In conversation, in meetings, in the street, in the hall, in the home, on the train, in the boat, he has stood for the whole Gospel!

In strength and in weakness, in health and in sickness, in joy and in sorrow, he has stood up for the Gospel of Christ.

God has honored him in making him one of the world's greatest soul winners who, as the stars, shall shine forever and ever, on earth and in Heaven.

COMMISSIONER BRENGLE HAS STOOD UP FOR THE SALVATION ARMY.

In this respect he is before us tonight with a conscience void of offense.

It cost him something to be a Salvationist.

It has cost him a great deal more to remain one.

HE HAS STOOD UP FOR ITS AUTHORITY.

It is very distressing to see any man taking the benefits of an organization or a society, accepting its honors at the same time criticizing its methods and belittling its authority. This is despicable in any sphere of life. It is despicable in the clerk of a bank who takes the privileges conferred on him by the manager and tries to belittle his authority behind his back. You will never find this ugly stain on the skirts of Commissioner Brengle.

He has stood up for the authority of the Army, defending its methods to the high and to the low, in universities and in slums, faithfully supporting in word and deed its leaders.

This faithfulness to the Army, coupled with his wisdom, his enlightened mind, educated and up to date on all matters relative to conditions, men, religion and the Army, has made his example a stronghold, a hiding place in storm, to the foremost officers under our flag.

The Founder, the late General Bramwell Booth, the Commander, have said, especially in times of trouble, "Where's Brengle? Send for Brengle."

No one can ever say what Commissioner Brengle has been to me in times of trouble.

HE HAS STOOD BEFORE THE WHOLE WORLD BRIGHT IN THE LIGHT OF AN UNSTINTED, UNDIMINISHING DEVOTION TO GOD.

No interest of family, of self-gain, or even of his work has he permitted to come between him and his God.

This has given to the Commissioner a divine quality of spirit which has made him a shining example even to religious leaders, both in and out of the Army, and has given to multitudes, low and high, rich and poor, a confidence in his teaching and in his judgment in spiritual matters which is unsurpassed.

From his heart, from his life and his teachings, there has flowed a continual spring of living water for thirsty souls wherever his influence has come.

COMMISSIONER BRENGLE HAS STOOD ALWAYS FOR THE GOOD OF OTHERS.

Through the years he has carried with him a realization of his obligation to do good to all men.

Whether talking with the Commander in her office, with a businessman, with a worldling, or with a poor debased soul of the street, he has always stood a brother to man, and remembered that OUR ONE FATHER IS GOD.

This is the "love of Christ" which recognizes no distinction of race or merit or rank.

COMMISSIONER BRENGLE STANDS AS A GLISTENING EXAMPLE FOR HOLY LITERATURE.

The pen is the lever that moves the world.

From the hour of the invention of the printing press, books and not kings have ruled the world, and I believe that weapons formed in the mind and heart of man--clean, holy and keen-edged--will not only supplant the sword and the cannon but will open up the gates of truth and righteousness to every thinking man.

Commissioner Brengle's pen has certainly moved the world. He has proved to readers of his books that beautiful literature springs from the fullness of intellectual, moral and spiritual life; from a depth of thought and emotion that can only derive their energy and sustenance from the religion of Jesus Christ.

COMMISSIONER BRENGLE HAS STOOD UP AS ONE OF THE WORLD'S GREATEST PREACHERS.

That man should profit in divine knowledge, faith, holiness, joy and love has been the end of all his preaching.

He has sought the salvation of the people, not his own glory. He has stood up against sin. In every class of society, small or great, high or low, before the young and before the old, he has stood up against sin.

He has called upon God to help him. Prayer has been the breath of his life, the pulse of his soul, the well from which he has drawn the glistening waters of his daily salvation and the Redeemer's fullness of power.

The General's tribute to the late Mrs. Commissioner Richard E. Holz

Mrs. Holz served with courage and distinction as Captain Mary Powell, and later joined her husband in reuniting the divided Armies at Saratoga Springs in 1889.

From The War Cry (Chicago) January 30, 1937.

Dear Mrs. Commissioner Holz is in the Gloryland! The news came to me here in Ceylon as a distinct personal shock and sense of heartfelt loss, for she has been a devoted comrade and friend for so many years.

The King's chariot has halted at our gates and taken from the ranks a warrior woman, a cheery personality, beloved and victorious.

For more than half a century she served her God in The Salvation Army with a largeness of heart that overflowed with Christlike love for the most needy, sinful and sorrowing.

In the days when poverty, persecution, misunderstanding and calumny were so largely a part of a Salvationist's life, she proved her priceless worth and fearlessly showed an unquenchable love for the lost and an heroic daring in preaching the Evangel to them.

From the very first years of her officership she proved herself one of the most active and fearless of women. Hers was a shining character, the whole structure of which was built on God. She loved righteousness. She proved herself a true-hearted comrade, not afraid to bear the burden, never shirking to carry the cross.

I shall miss the force of her prayers and the invigorating influence of her buoyant faith. God's presence, God's guidance and the reality of God's power were, for her, blessed realities.

A great torrent of tender and understanding sympathy flows from my heart to dear Commissioner Holz and members of the family. I know that Salvationists everywhere will join me in heartfelt prayer that divine support be granted them, and that Heaven's promised light of His consolation may transform the shadow, which their dear one's passing has cast on their way, into gold, making more clearly defined than ever the path to the skies.

The heavenly gates have opened and a beloved comrade has stepped into the light of eternal peace. We do not catch the burst of heavenly song that greeted her, yet we know that her entrance was more than abundant--"Washed in the Blood of the Lamb."

She is now triumphant over life's battles; conqueror over sin, suffering and the grave. She sings with the blood-washed throng in the Eternal City. But the inspiration of her life, so rich in influence and abundant in sacrifice, will never die.

If we are faithful, if we are true, if we endure to the end, we shall meet her in the morning in that tearless land where all is joy for evermore, for Jesus the Christ is there.

ECB's four adopted children, Pearl, Jhai, Dot and Willie

ECB astride her horse, Golden Heart

ECB with her father, William Booth, Founder of the Salvation Army

ECB with her brother, Bramwell Booth, second General of The Salvation Army

Photographs supplied by National Archives and Research Center, Alexandria, Virginia; George Scott Railton Heritage Centre, Toronto, Ontario and Commissioner John D. Waldron (R)

Colonel William Evans: An Appreciation

An address at the retirement of Colonel William Evans, with "a brief sketch of the veteran officer's career."

From The War Cry (New York) March 1, 1924.

For forty years Colonel and Mrs. William Evans have been in the foreranks of Salvation Army service. From the time when, in their early youth, they dedicated themselves under its Flag to the preaching of the Gospel, the salvation of souls and the betterment of the world, with unfaltering purpose they have maintained their allegiance, justified the confidence reposed in them by their leaders and steadily risen to more and more important and responsible positions. The range of work to which the Colonel has been assigned has afforded the fullest scope for his exceptional gifts, and again and again the sterling qualities of character of both have found expression in substantial and lasting achievements in connection with the spiritual, as well as the material progress of the Army.

Colonel Evans came out of York, England, in 1883, and about a year later was sent over to America, where he immediately plunged into the pioneer work of those early and troublous years. He shared in the hardship, the ridicule, the persecution and the bitter poverty of the first days of the Army in America, but he shared also in the flaming zeal, the conquering faith and the fire of love for souls that kept our comrades up and carried them on singlehanded to victory in the face of a thousand foes.

These fires have never died down in the Colonel's heart, their light has never gone out.

Rare Tact, Patience and Inspiring Zest

After a few months as a corps officer in the city of Syracuse, the needs of the war took him to Western New York as a Divisional Officer, since which time he has been engaged exclusively in positions of leadership as Divisional Officer, Provincial Officer and Chief Secretary. With rare tact and patience, yet with inspiring zest and belligerent wisdom he has filled the places assigned to him, and the hundreds of officers over whom from time to time he has been placed have cheerfully followed his daring faith and zeal. He was the first to introduce the Lightning Campaign as a means of raising the funds for important building schemes. In this he enjoyed a notable success.

While no regular appointment has been held by the Colonel for some little time, owing to the unsatisfactory condition of his own and Mrs. Evans' health, this has not prevented his rendering much useful service and, while he is now entering upon the quieter, yet not less useful or happy years of a well earned retirement, it is hoped that for a long time to come he will continue to undertake similar lines of service in all parts of the country.

On behalf of the General, and of the entire American Staff and Field, I am glad to express our gratitude to God for Colonel and Mrs. Evans' forty years of victorious and holy service under the Flag of The Salvation Army, and to assure them that our prayers will follow them.

"Did you ever, by accident, break a thermometer-glass and see the quicksilver run? Pretty lively stuff, eh? Well, take say, 150 pounds of it, shape it into human similitude, dress it in Salvation Army uniform and, if it were possible to breathe the breath of a sturdy spiritual and physical life into it, you would have Colonel William Evans duplicated to a nicety."

This original cameo of the man, Salvationist and warrior, Colonel Evans, as drawn by a *War Cry* chronicler of twenty years ago, was characteristically representative of the entire life and untiring fighting of this veteran of a thousand battles and as many victories in the Salvation War.

He was indeed "ever on the alert, taking short cuts, dodging under horses' heads, taking the street if he finds the sidewalk clogged with pedestrians, leaping on a disappearing car while other people are waiting for the next one--working while others think; thinking while others sleep." He was a genius for work, and it was often said of him that he was one of those men who obey the new commandment, "Six days shalt thou labor, and do double duty on the seventh," for nothing delighted the Colonel's soldier heart more than a full Sunday's battle for souls, regardless of how full of other duties the week had been, and the predominant passion of his whole life's work was the desire to see men and women born into the Kingdom of God.

To attempt anything like a life sketch of Colonel Evans today, after he has spent more than two score years fighting under the Blood-and-Fire Banner of the Army, would be, as remarked by the writer we mentioned before, "like carrying coals to Newcastle or beef to Chicago."

The Colonel's full and fruitful life has been an integral part of the growth and success of The Salvation Army in the United States.

Several weeks ago Commissioner Thomas Estill conducted the fortieth anniversary celebration of the opening of Salvation Army operations in Buffalo, N.Y., and it was there related by the Chief Secretary, Colonel Richard E. Holz, that as a young man he had stood among the crowd which gathered for the first meeting conducted there by two youthful Salvationists, of whom Captain William Evans, as he was then, was the commanding officer. They knelt in the snow and prayed, and sang the battlesongs of the Army, and the Flag they planted there is still flying.

So it has been in innumerable cities, and to write the account of the career of Colonel Evans would be to report the steady onward march of The Salvation Army from the Atlantic to the Pacific and recount the scores of victories, tell of the hard fights and persecutions, chronicle again the many struggles; in short, compile a detailed history of the advance of the movement in America during the past forty years, for, with the exception of the first three or four brief years of the Army's history here, Colonel William Evans has been conspicuously at the front of the battle and in a large measure directing or assisting in the direction of the fight.

And it was a fight--a fight that meant bloodshed and discouragement, imprisonment and the bitterest persecution and disheartening misunderstanding, but a fight victorious.

The Colonel was born on September 23, 1859--six years before the birth of the now worldwide Salvation Army in the first meeting conducted on Mile-End Waste in London by the Rev. William Booth. His father and mother, Mr. and Mrs. Richard Evans, were living in York--old York, the city of the famed York Minster and Cathedral in the Old Country, and it was from the York Corps that he went to training as a cadet for officership in the Army.

Richard Evans, his father, so well known to American Salvationists as "Dad" Evans, was also a battlescarred veteran, whose name was a household word with Salvationists from Maine to California. But when William first made his acquaintance he was enjoying prosperity as the proprietor of a brass foundry.

William was the only child of his parents, and "Mother" Evans first gave him to God, and then to the Army, away back in the days when the organization was without form and certainly without prestige. And this great trait of self-sacrifice and abandonment to the will and service of God was also characteristic of the life and career of her son.

He was sent from the Training College as Captain in charge of the important corps at Woolwich, the great arsenal city of England, but in a few months was sent to America.

Coming to America in 1883, one of the first events that occurred after Captain Evans' landing was his marriage to Captain Hannah Simpson in New York.

This, by the way, was the very first Salvation Army wedding in this country.

It will be seen that in this, as in so many other things, the Colonel occupied a historic position, and set the pace for future generations. He had met Captain Simpson in York, England, before he married her in New York, America. At that time she was Lieutenant to Captain Malthouse, one of our veteran Field Officers, and Evans was merely a soldier. Our readers must fill in the blanks themselves.

The Army work had only been established in America for two or three years. The Evanses, following their wedding, struck out for Syracuse, N.Y. and came very near having to spend their honeymoon in jail for marching the streets with the corps.

Those were the days of real pioneering, when the mighty Goliaths of misunderstanding and bitter prejudice had to be faced, wrestled with and overthrown. Six months here were followed by a term at Buffalo, where, as we have already intimated, our present Chief Secretary was numbered among the 500 converts that lined the mercy-seat during the first six weeks.

Here it was that promotion to Divisional Officership came, and then the appointment to open up the work in the West, with Chicago as the base of operations.

The tug at his mother's heart of the boy so far away finally drew father and mother across the ocean after they had closed their business interests in the old land.

Freed from other interests and feeling the pressing need for officers, father and mother offered themselves for officership in the Army. They were accepted and were sent under the command of their son.

During a considerable period of this time the Colonel's father was an able A.D.C. to him, and did admirable scout duty for years throughout the great Northwest.

The Colonel's mother was one of the sweetest spirits and most devoted women officers the Army has ever known.

In the West Colonel Evans' Territory was semi-continental, and during his memorable command corps were opened up in the States of Illinois, Kansas, Nebraska, Iowa, Missouri, Minnesota, Wisconsin and Arkansas.

This, of course, was a history-making command. It was virgin soil that was being broken up. Those days were days of foundation-stone laying, the importance of which cannot well be overestimated, and their record is numbered among the Colonel's greatest triumphs and was achieved because of his tact and courage in the face of most trying difficulties.

The roster of names of men and women sent into the work by the Colonel is an extraordinarily long one, including, among the most prominent Staff Officers, Colonel Richard Holz, the Chief Secretary, Colonel Edward J. Parker, Territorial Men's Social Secretary and Colonel Benjamin Nelson, in charge of the Scandinavian Department for the Eastern Territory.

Colonel Evans was at one time the Chief Secretary for the United States, and his successful career as the leader of Salvation Army activities in the Pacific Coast Division, the New England Province and the old Ohio and Kentucky Province, is so thoroughly known to his many, many comrades throughout the country as to render a recapitulation scarcely necessary. It was characterized by the same intensity of push and "go"--the same faculty for originating new plans and working them to a successful issue--that has marked the Colonel as a man among men.

But we must not intimate in the least that his career is among those requiring the past tense of the verb. He is still the same energetic, never tiring, true blue, blood-and-fire Salvationist and is not content unless actively engaging the enemy at the very front line of the battle.

His last active appointment was as Provincial Officer for the Ohio and Kentucky Province, with Headquarters at Pittsburgh. He entered this command July 1, 1908, and led it forward with great strides until, on October 1, 1920, he was forced to relinquish all active responsibility and go on furlough, owing to the very poor condition of Mrs. Evans' health.

Last Summer they spent several weeks in England, visiting old friends and comrades there, especially their daughter Eva--Mrs. Major Edward P. Higgins, wife of the Divisional Commander for the West Yorks Division, England.

Their family consists of four children--three daughters and one son: Lizzie, the eldest, wife of Lt. Colonel Samuel Withers, Divisional Commander for the Michigan Division; Eva, who is Mrs. Edward Higgins; Myrtle, wife of Ensign William Gearing, Divisional Young People's Secretary for the Southern Division; and the youngest and the only son, Willard, recently appointed Divisional Young People's Secretary for the Chesapeake Division.

Dearest Susie (Susie Forrest Swift)

A personal letter to the former Brigadier Susie Forrest Swift, sometime editor of All the World magazine, contributor to other Army periodicals and outstanding woman officer in the Army's early days.

This is being reproduced as it originally appeared in Evangeline's own handwriting (together with a typed transcript).

Discovered among the private papers of Sister Imelda Teresa Swift, in the National Headquarters Archives, then in New York City.

NEW YORK 11.24.12

Dearest Susie.

I have been carrying your letter around with me ever since it came into my hands upon my return from London. waiting for the moment

to write you with
my own hand.

It was just
like your old dear
-ness to write
me and your words
dropped into their
old preserved place
in my changeless
heart.

The loss of.

my precious father has
almost shattered me
I can't yet realize it.
As I think you know he
was *everything* to me -
after God I lived for him
thought for him. worked
for him. and so yet I can-
-not realize he is no
more with me *here*.

But oh the wonder
of the depth of meaning
in those words
"*I shall not want*".
Gods tender compassion
and understanding *pity*
can touch and heal every
wound of the human heart.
and although our sorrows
make a difference and

NEW YORK

we never feel the
same may be we
are better as the
storms alter the
hills and the great
trees. bending some
and spreading
others but giving
to nature a touch
of greater magnifi-
cence.

How are you?

I would love to see you. You were always so good to me — I wish I had you helping me now. My burdens are very heavy.

In prayer and love unchanging

Evangeline Booth

E.C.B. - New York - 11.22.12

Dear Susie:

I have been carrying your letter around with me ever since it came into my hands upon my return from London, waiting for the moment to write you with my own pen.

It was just like your old dearness to write me, and your words stepped into their old preserved place in my changeless heart.

The loss of my precious father has almost shattered me. I can't yet realize it. As I think you know, he was **everything to me**. After God, I lived for him, thought for him, worked for him and as yet I cannot realize he is no more with me **here**.

But--Oh the wonder of the depth of meaning in those words, "**I shall not want**."

God's tender compassion and understanding **pity** can touch and heal every wound of the human heart and, although our sorrows make a difference and we never feel the same, maybe we are better as the storms alter the hills and the great trees, bending some and spreading others, but giving to nature a touch of greater magnificence.

How are you? I would love to see you. You were always so good to me. I wish I had you helping me now--my burdens are **very heavy**.

In prayer and love **unchanging**,

Evangeline Booth

A Grand Old Warrior and Saint Passes Through the Gates Eternal

A tribute to Commissioner Frederick Booth-Tucker on his promotion to Glory, with a brief sketch of his life.

From The War Cry (New York) August 17, 1929.

Commissioner Booth-Tucker has been a star bright and shining in the sky of The Salvation Army. Men of all lands have looked up to it and have gone the braver and the better upon their way.

His face, his form, his name and the saintly character of his life are perhaps better known than any follower of our Flag, apart from our Founder. And the gap made in our long columns by his quick summons Home makes the heart of the numberless thousands to whom he brought light and healing desolate.

To be wanted back when you have forever gone, to be loved and reverenced by the peoples of the earth because of the sacrifice you made for them, is in itself a crown. And although ever effacing himself, and for over thirty years in the darkness of India, gratitude and honor of countless numbers of the world over placed this imperishable token upon the sainted brow.

Booth-Tucker was our great pathfinder. He was the first under our banner to carry the torch of the Gospel into the mental and spiritual fog of heathendom. He showed the way to win the hearts of those who sit in darkness. He made the heathen, the most ignorant, the most repulsive his brother. The imprint of his feet down the ways of a million sacrifices and toils unseen by the eye of man, will remain until the sands in the desert grow cold and the Books of the Judgment unfold.

He had the mind, the limitless enthusiasm, the courage and the spirit of the emancipator. Never for a moment did he lose sight of the goal for the good of all. Adamant in purpose--never hesitating to count the cost--any minute as ready to die as to live.

While fearlessly brave in contention for the right, he manifested the highest Christian virtues under every circumstance. The foundation of his faith growing stronger with the years, all his glory was in Christ as the Redeemer of men, which made him to love above all else the mercy-seat until his triumphant finish. Commissioner Booth-Tucker in the highest and truest sense of the word was a soldier and a saint.

In the United States his name will never die. At a period in its history he displayed the courage, faith and skill in administration that marked him a prophet of God.

The loss to his beloved wife and precious children is great indeed. The wounds will be long open, but the Savior will not leave them alone a single minute. In the arms of His grace He will comfort them.

I shall miss him greatly. He was a friend. He was a brother. He was a counselor. In many a dark hour of fierce fighting he has been a bulwark of strength and comfort.

You will miss him. The world will miss him. His spirit was a benediction. His pen a mighty power. He won for himself honor and reverence and love of the Salvationists all over the world.

Farewell! It is hard, this parting, one by one, with our fondly loved comrades, with whom we have stood from youngest years in numberless battles.

But farewell, brother and friend. You have gone beyond the sound of our voices and the sight of our faces, but not beyond the beat of our hearts. You will meet the Founder, by whom you were so dearly beloved, and others who will greet you with outstretched arms. But greatest and grandest and dearest of all you will meet your own spiritual children from many lands with the light of the face of their Redeemer upon them.

Farewell till we meet again!

Let our thoughts upon the life and death of Commissioner Booth-Tucker take us out of the rut of today, away from our own selfish cares. Let them for a brief period even break in upon thoughts concentrated upon plans and schemes for our own work and arrest even laudable endeavors for our own greater achievements.

Let the passing through the gates eternal of this grand old warrior and saint stop the wheel of our activities for a short period and force us to think of our ancestors. To think upon those who stood in the first lines of the first days, will do us good--their countless toils, their real personal sacrifices, their teasing and nerve-taxing annoyances, their battle with opposition, with poverty, with false accusations, with stonings and imprisonment and with sorrow--sorrows of suffering and death without monetary help to meet the claims of sickness and burial and, owing to the Army's cramped numbers in their day, very little sympathy, for their tears and pains were unheard of.

It is a good thing for us to revive the memory of our own history and let our hearts dwell upon the heroes of its making, that we may be filled with a noble appreciation of the virtues and glories of our fathers--those who have gone before us laying the foundations of our great organization and establishing our unparalleled reputation of individual sacrifice to the Cross of Christ and our service to the lowly and love for the worst.

The calling from our lines of this saint for his crowning should cause us to examine our own conscience. He has left our organization a mighty legacy in the imperishable blessings of his religion.

From the time he made his choice to be a savior of men when a Judge of the Civil Service in India and became a missionary, sacrificing comfort and plenty, to live as a native that he might win the natives for God, clothing himself in the humblest native costume, going barefooted, eating native food and for many years begging it from door to door, he never withdrew his eyes from the Cross and its burden of blood and agony for a world's salvation.

In secret, in public, at home and abroad he always brought before me the vision of a man butting against a storm to reach the goal, ever pressing forward, never hesitating, never looking to the side, never turning back. Always on, on, on to get nearer to the one great Example who controlled every thought and passion and ambition of his being.

Prayer with Commissioner Booth-Tucker was a momently communion with his Lord. The light of the spirit of truth revealed the right and the wrong with every step of the journey.

He loved much, because he was all love. He gave much, because there was nothing left that he did not give. He worked much, because this was his only means of joy. Age, weariness and even pain--as far as possible claiming consideration--tempted him to impatience.

He had a master spirit--a spirit which seemed to rise above all others around him and cast its influence upon you, all imperceptible to himself.

There is the legacy of his character. The most distinguished Frenchman of his century said, "Men succeed less by their talents than their character." There have been scores of men through the years who had more intellect than Washington, who were more clever than Lincoln, but these men override them all by the imperishable influence of character.

Commissioner Booth-Tucker was such a luminous and strong character that his influence was not alone for his lifetime or for those who knew him intimately, but its radiance spreads all over the world and is a continuous, progressive and never-ending agency for good.

He was strong. He had the strength of genius. But he, as with all true geniuses, could be subdued and convinced by higher reason. However, his train of thought and conviction never changed by pleas of cowardice, self-gain, or praise. These things he passed by as the runner of a marathon passes side avenues.

As always with the genius he was a creator--a man who found his own road and carried his own lamp, but ever ready to lend the light of his brain or his tongue or his hands or his heart to a fellow traveler. I never have known Commissioner Booth-Tucker to refuse help to the smallest or to the greatest--help of his inimitable pen; help of giving a thought to a speaker called hurriedly upon in a great meeting; help of a paragraph in the public press of defense for the humblest cause; help given by hidden toil; help of letters written in the night hour, hurrying spiritual advice or consolation, only read by the eye of the one to whom addressed and the eye of God.

To me, speaking for myself, his character stands up pinnacle-like for the eyes of all Salvationists all over the world, for their children and their children's children to look upon and be blessed thereby.

He left us the example of his humble walking before the Lord. Saint as he was, he had an innate aversion to be thought or referred to in the slightest way as any better than any other man. This gave to him an exceptional modesty of speaking of even the blessing of God that crowned his public efforts. Unless he could cover his personal connection with the occasion, he would prefer it passed unnoticed.

He was a genius. He had the weaknesses of the genius, if such they can be called--the impatience of the genius. Genius is always impatient of its harness. Its wild free blood makes it hard to hold. He was ofttimes unwilling to weigh the pros and cons, the possible loss as well as the possible profit of the invention, the scheme, the thought. He was not an organizer, a systematizer, a man of details. With the stride of the great he was apt to swing by these things and leave them to others, and there are always plenty of others whose capacities reach thus far.

But Booth-Tucker was a creator, and India and America will ever stand as the greatest debtors to his life. He started in this country, the United States, a work for the uplift of man and glory of God that has revolutionized The Salvation Army in this and other lands, multiplied past estimate, the good we can do; augmented the service and efforts and talents of the small man almost past calculation; a work that will go until the angel standing with one foot on the sea and the other on the earth shall cry, "Time shall be no more!"

From the hour he consecrated himself and life to God, until the hour he rendered his commission to the hand that gave it, he paid the full price through the long, toiling journey of his service to merit the "Well done."

These memories must make our feet to hasten, our spirits to be earnest and watchful that the prayers of the sages and the saints of our banner of the various nations of the world shall be answered; and that all those who pass from us leaving the white record behind them, shall make our organization more clearly to show forth the glory of our Father in Heaven by the wondrous work of the heart and the hand of His children on earth.

Chapter Five

The Salvation Army

Sacrificial Hands

The story of the beginnings of the Order of the Silver Star

From The War Cry (Toronto) May 8, 1937.

Only one thing in the world is better than a good wife--that is a good mother. From the very beginning of all until the very end of all a mother is the dearest and holiest thing alive. The first impressions made upon the awakening intelligence of the babe is always her work. The future destiny of the child is her work. And if there is anything on earth that outreaches the human, in thought, in deed, in word, in suffering, in endurance and in sacrifice, it is a mother's love.

Thus I thought as through the hours of the night there came back to me the strong features of the young officer--his breadth of shoulder, his height of 6 feet odd, and his unmistakable evidence of clear thinking--who told me of the sacrifice of his widow mother. With three little girls yet to bring up, she had refused to withhold him from officership in The Salvation Army.

He had said to me: "For every word of congratulation I received for giving the advantages of my education to the work I say in my heart, 'Mother, this is for you.' When I was promoted to the rank of Adjutant, I said, 'Mother, this Silver Star is yours.' The kind words of appreciation which you have spoken to me this morning are all my mother's. The immortal souls whom God has enabled me to show the way from misery and bleakness of soul to the paths of pardon and peace will be among the jewels in her crown."

And, so I thought, he has not forgotten. He has a sweet wife, a young son, he is absorbed in his work, but he has not forgotten his mother.

When his eyes, with the restrained tears, came before me in the night hours, I saw long lines of mothers who, with sacrificial hands, had laid their children upon the altar of service of The Salvation Army, that they might be winners of the souls of men. From this vision came the thought of the Silver Star.

This badge of honor means also that the dear mothers who have given their children to be officers in the ranks of the Army must do more to help other mothers to give theirs. This star, worn upon their breasts, will be a call sweet and lasting to thousands who have never before thought that God asked this same gift of them.

I want the Silver Star mothers to know that this Order has been founded upon my inexpressible gratitude. I remember my own mother--the Army's Mother. Many Silver Star mothers will remember her. Through the long years her face comes before me, clear, vivid, with a preciousness that alone can be spoken of as incomparable and infinite; her eyes, two bottomless pools of mercy and understanding, but two quenchless flames when face to face with the oppressor.

There were eight of us, but not one was neglected. The path was clearly marked for our feet.

I would point out to the Army's mothers that love for your sons or daughters falls pitiably short if you desire for them no greater things than those material advantages which, as you yourself as a Salvationist proclaim, can never satisfy the soul.

It has been well said that "No mother can place her children upon a higher plane than that upon which she herself stands. The children may reach it, but it will not be through her."

It is the Salvationist's mission--particularly the mission of Army mothers--to make it clear to their children that we have come into the world to make it better, that we have been laid down at the Cross for that purpose, that before our children could give themselves we, their parents, gave them to Christ, that they might make better the world for which He died.

The Order of the Silver Star has, too, come from the love of mothers for me. A thousand times this has been my strength. A thousand times this has nerved my heart. A thousand times this has made me smile when I would have wept, and held up my head when it would have bowed low beneath the weight of sorrow and misunderstanding that came upon me.

If I bring you any comfort by the Order of the Silver Star, why--you have fastened in my sky a thousand stars that can never grow dim! My love will ever be yours.

* * * * *

Our Flags Victorious

A reflection on the flags of the United States and The Salvation Army.

From The War Cry (New York) July 4, 1908.

Salute the Flag! The schoolchild's hand is lifted and the sweet young treble adds its tribute to the standard to which all its future is pointed.

Salute the Flag! The barren staff blossoms into red, white and blue, and every military sleeve rises to respect before the pride of the hour.

Salute the Flag! The dim eye brightens and some of the old firmness returns to the veteran's step as the G.A.R. battalion forms before the symbol which enwraps all the most precious memories of the past.

What true patriot's heart does not beat higher as the Flag waves into view? What true patriot's soul does not swell with aspiration to lift and defend the glorious principles with which its folds are interwoven?

There is no need for me, at this late day, to deliver a eulogy upon the national emblem of freedom. This has been done--and done sufficiently and well--over and over again by men of national celebrity on the anniversary of American independence which gave to this great country a separate name and identity. No need for me to hark back to those troublous times, but rather to thank God that they are long since over, and that so much that is good and great has at every epoch in our young nation's career followed in the wake of its standard.

Symbolism of the Flag

Since assuming command of The Salvation Army's interests in this country, a question has arisen in my mind as to whether the statesmen who in the first place chose the form and design of the National Flag were altogether unmindful of its suggestive symbolism. So striking is this that it suggests to my own mind that some inspiration coupled the *stars* with the *stripes*! What more powerful, what more mighty, what more forcible demonstration of the well-attested fact that the reward comes by the royal road of suffering--that before the *stars* can be gained the *stripes* must be borne! It will do us good, my comrades, to think of this significance of the Flag when we watch its graceful folds waving in the breeze, until for us every flagpole may prove a pulpit and each individual star and stripe a preacher of God's truth.

A victorious Flag, truly, is the Stars and Stripes. It has received its baptism of blood upon which it is not necessary for me to dwell in detail, and an all-wise Providence has permitted it to come through with the thrill and throb of victory interwoven with its every strand.

Another Flag

The artist has intertwined another Flag with the National Standard--another Flag not only christened in blood, but sanctified by the agonized tears and stifling sobs of ten thousand penitents.

The tricolor of The Salvation Army!
"The Flag that guides poor sinners on the way,
The Flag that leads to endless day,
The Flag that fills all Hell with dismay--
The Flag of The Salvation Army."

The Flag whose heart of gold speaks of the sacred consuming fire of the Holy Ghost, and whose crimson and blue tell of the purity wrought in us and purchased for us by the precious blood of Calvary's Fount.

The Flag that has become a sacred thing to us through its association with innumerable spiritual conflicts in which we have played a part, and I hope played it well.

The Flag under which precious Army babes are given to God and the blessed War, and bright young comrades pledge their troth to each other and to the fight "for better or worse." The Flag which every one of us hopes to have draped over our dying pillow as the last goodbyes are said, and in our departing soul the assurances of the covenanted mercy it represents as we await the summons to the muster of the righteous before the Throne.

"Under the Army Flag we'll fight our way to glory,
Under the Army Flag we'll conquer or we'll die;
Under the Army Flag we'll tell salvation's story;
'Victory and Salvation!' shall be our battle cry."

True, it has been attacked, spat upon, wrenched from its staff, drenched with the slime and ooze of the gutter, spattered with bad eggs and worse vegetables, tattered and torn in the fray, but these things to us have an altogether different meaning than to a great many people. They not only speak to us of the scoff and jibe and jeer of the giddy, godless multitude, but point to the apostolic character of our efforts. As long as the world is the world and sin is sin and self is self, there will still be the "Shame of the Cross," and our precious Flag as its representative has in past days again and again been the butt of keen ridicule and of fierce opposition.

Heroic deeds have been done and warrior veins have been opened in the defense of the Blood-and-Fire Flag and the world embracing salvation for which it stands. Our people have been hounded like dogs, haled to the courts as malefactors and assailed by every missile and mistreatment with which fiendish hatred and lie can belabor Love and Truth. But they have triumphed even when martyr's death has sealed their fidelity, and by the hand of the faithful the flag has been lifted and carried higher for such affronts to the standard-bearer. All honor to the heroes of The Salvation Army Flag! Their names may never find recognition at the hands of a world's fame, but their deeds will not go unrecorded in the Pantheon of the Skies.

Always Victorious

But it has always come out victorious, nevertheless! Its poor fabric might have been torn to shreds, as it has been in many cases, but the glorious foundation principles it represents have invariably won and will go on winning for all time.

"The Flag that will ever in battle look bright,
The Flag that will wave till the wrong is put right:
The Flag that shall triumph with salvation might,
Is the Flag of The Salvation Army."

It is going to continue a conquering flag. We Salvationists care little for tradition. The past, good as it may have been in conquest and victory, is incomparable with the mighty present and future. It is not to unlock the doors of the barred and finished past that our hearts pine for, but rather to insert the key of unflagging, tireless zeal in the golden lock of opportunity that the future places before us. May God help us!

We must do more marching.

We must do more praying.

We must do more believing.

We must do more fighting.

We must live lives of less self-consciousness and greater abandonment to the principles of the Flag.

Units make a crowd.

Individual soldiers constitute an army.

You count for one, and must bear the responsibility of one, and war the warfare of one, and bear the cross and crucifixion of one, and then receive the reward and enjoy the welcome home of a true soldier.

You Can Help!

You can help make the Flag more than ever victorious in the days to come. Our fight is a "more and more" fight.

Always a little more to be done! The task never finished! The minions of sin are tireless. Death and destruction follow in their wake. Their task is never finished, nor can ours be! God give us strength to perform it!

Thank God there is likewise "always more grace." "Always more strength." His storehouse is boundless. It is ever at our command. Blest be His name!

One thing, it seems to me, the Flag tells us we must not do is grow weary of the fight--get listless, disheartened at opposition, discouraged perhaps at lack of definite results, thus seriously entertaining the thought of retiring from the fray.

"I cannot leave the dear old Flag,
'Twere better far to die!"

It is not the dying veteran who is filled with vain regrets. To him comes the opening to vistas of glory, hitherto only dreamed of. It is the deserter, the traitor, who will have to be content with a slinking, doglike experience, despised by all, held in contempt by God and man alike.

My call to you, my beloved comrades, is for a breaking away from every last vestige of self-seeking, a wholehearted renunciation of all that savors of the ordinary and conventional in spiritual life and a final and utter abandonment to the wonderful and mighty principles our Flag waves before us. If the Stars and Stripes speaks to us of our opportunity, surely the Salvation Army Flag reminds us of our responsibility. May we not fall short of the service to which these intertwined colors would call us!

Guardians of the Covenant

A charge to the Cadets of the Guardians of the Covenant Session commissioned in Royal Albert Hall, May 3, 1937. It was the General's expressed desire "that it should be regarded by the Cadets of the 1937-38 sessions everywhere as addressed equally to each."

Published by the Campfield Press, St. Albans, England (undated).

My Dear Cadets:

This is a great day in your history. I think--apart from the day upon which there dawned the morning of your salvation--this is the greatest day that will ever come to you, for it is the day upon which you pass through the gates of your officership in the worldwide Salvation Army. It is the day when you push off from the shores of the loving and protecting harbor of the Training College upon the seas of service over which you must navigate your own voyage.

I remember when this day came to me. My commission was handed to me by my father. My recollection of the occasion is so vivid that my whole being thrills as I think upon it. My fingers never felt quite the same holding anything before, nor have they since, as when I took that simple but momentous document from his dear hand. They felt as though they entwined around something of heaven as well as earth, of eternity as well as time.

And so I came to take up the responsibility of my first independent Command. It was a forlorn hope in the Slums, but it seemed to me so large--so important! A vision of the little place rises before my eyes now; the small dingy room--the bare board floor, the bedstead--and two chairs! Holding the commission with my two hands over my rapidly pulsating heart I prayed. No, it was not a prayer. It was an impassioned plea! It was not a request. It was an importunate demand! It was not the expression of a divine hope. It was the declaration of an all dominating faith! It was not a sweet and calm entreaty. It was a stormy outpouring in which throbbed the energy of my whole being! It was a call to the Throne of God!

I did not ask alone for love that I might enfold all the earth in blessing; not alone for grace that in my life might be exemplified all the beatitudes; not alone for patience that I might bear and forbear; not alone for triumph that over the fierce conflicts of my battlefields I might hear the shout of triumph; not alone even for the crowded Penitent Forms for which my soul thirsted. My impassioned entreaty was that I might be kept. Kept strong, kept brave, kept faithful, kept true. Kept! Kept from making shipwreck, so that at the end I might be saved. Cadets! This was my prayer, that, having sworn to my own hurt, I should change not!

Seasons of spiritual import and historic interest have come to me since then; battles hard and desperate, their issues fraught with momentous importance to The Salvation Army; victories, the ringing cheers of which can never be forgotten. But no season stands out more vividly in my memory, more precious in its recollections, more complete in its consecration, or more desperate in its demanding faith, than that day.

Now this day has come to you; the day upon which you receive your first commission for the sacred and important position of an officer in The Salvation Army. In the name of Him who has called you to the office; by the heroic warfare and blameless example of a multitude of officers of our worldwide Army who have gone before you; by the thousand toils and hopes and expectations of the Principal and Staff of the Training College; by ten thousand prayers of loved ones--mothers, fathers--who sent you forth; by the desperate needs and sorrow and sins of the people who await your ministry, I charge you, be faithful Guardians of the Covenant into which you have entered.

I commission you for the one great mission to which you were called: to preach Christ and Him crucified! In this day of attack upon the Christian faith; this day of seductive and pernicious teaching; this day of contradiction of the Word of God; this day of the rebuttal of the story of Bethlehem--preach Him! Preach Jesus Christ!

Preach His birth. The manger, the shepherds, the wise men, the angelic announcement to the world of the nativity of the child King. Preach His boyhood: at twelve years of age confusing and confounding the professors in the Temple. Preach Him at Jacob's well, where with exquisite tact He revealed to the poor woman her soul's thirst and gave her the Water of Life. Preach Him meeting the widow of Nain and turning her mourning into song. Preach Him curing the lepers of their diseases and causing the lame to leap for joy as they threw away their crutches. Preach Him with His arms around the little children, their heads upon His breast, while they look into His lovely face. Preach Him in the boats of the fishermen, filling up their empty nets. Preach Him gathering the poor and the sick and the troubled and the hungry, and soothing all their sorrows.

My officers-to-be, I charge you: Preach His life! Preach His death! Preach Him falsely accused at the great tribunal, with pale face and silent lips! Preach Him praying in the Garden. The heart agony, the bloody sweat, the "Nevertheless, not My will but Thine be done!" Preach Him the victim of a traitor's diabolical plot! Preach Him thrust and pushed in the crowd, the blood surging from His temples, the hardstruck cheek, the stone-bruised feet, the shoulders bent low under the Cross burden. Preach Him suffering.

Preach Him dying on Calvary: His broken heart, His lacerated form, suffering and sorrow heaving up against His Cross in one wrathful, foaming, gory, omnipotent surge!

Preach the Risen Christ. Conqueror of sin and death, the Savior of all who will turn to Him, the all sufficient Keeper of those who put their trust in Him! Christ the Redeemer! Christ the King! Christ the everlasting Word, the Son of God, the Alpha and Omega, who was and is and ever shall be.

Preach Him! Preach Him!

I shall pray for you! I shall trust you.

Evangeline Booth

The Penitent-Form: Its Significance as a Sacred Place of Decision

From The War Cry (New York) October 9, 1937.

Many times I have given thought to the importance and work of The Salvation Army penitent-form. I have wondered whether our Salvationists recognize its real value in its relationship to the work, and whether we have come to regard it more lightly than we did a few years back.

Realizing its inestimable service from the hour of the Army's first stroke against sin, I feel the need to enforce its claims.

The penitent-form is a foundation method of The Salvation Army's work. It is the starting post of the Salvationist. It always has been and always will be.

The work done at the penitent-form is not an auxiliary. It is the cornerstone. It is not an afterthought.

The first breath of the movement was breathed at the penitent-form when the first penitent met his Savior there.

It is our first, chief and most powerful method of fulfilling the God-created purposes of the organization.

We did not start with a band; we did not start with the uniform or with poor men's hotels, or slum corps, but we *did* start with the penitent-form, in the dark of Mile-End Waste, London, where the Army was born.

It is not merely one of the many institutions of the Army; it is one of the vitals that can never, never change, and from which it can never be separated and live.

Here are some of the uses of the penitent-form: The penitent-form is, in one way, our altar. No altar is more sacred. It is the altar upon which have been laid the offerings of the soul and service of our people for God and His Kingdom.

It is the altar upon which have been laid the sacrifices of widows who have given their daughters; of fathers who have given their sons; upon which have been left the consecrations of men's souls--more precious to God than all the world's gifts.

The penitent-form is our baptismal font, where the fire of God's Spirit falls upon our soldiers.

There the live coals from off His altar consume their selfishness and sin; their love of ease and of the world; there the sanctifying wave of His Blood has drenched from their garments the last remains of sin, separating them from the world, the flesh and the devil.

The penitent-form is our communion rail, where the broken links of fellowship arc united; where grudge bearing has been lost, the enemy forgiven, the estranged ones reconciled.

The penitent-form at the foot of the Cross of Jesus is the gate at which the sinner, the oppressed, the wicked, have laid down their burdens; the pool where the most base, the most filthy, the most unloved, the most unwanted on earth, the most hungered for in Heaven, have been washed and made clean in the Blood flowing from the heart of the Lamb of God.

The penitent-form is our factory for ammunition.

Here the soldiers have found their zeal; here their sword has been resharpened; here the candidate has found courage to offer for the work; here differences in the home circle have been settled; here the wearing of the uniform is decided.

The Salvation Army penitent-form is the spiritual Waterloo of tens of thousands of souls. It covers all differences. It has made the saved heathen our brother. It has brought to the same level the rich and the poor, for The Salvation Army penitent-form is like the love of God: "Whosoever will may come."

The penitent-form has made us what we are. From it we get our soldiers. I do not say that all those who go to the penitent-form make soldiers. I only say that nearly all the soldiers we have come that way. Generally speaking, we have little faith in those who come to us through any other door.

See then, how much we owe to the penitent-form in our past and present; would it not be folly to suppose that the future does not equally depend upon it?

We are agreed upon its value to us. It furnishes our supplies. Let us see then if we cannot bring more people to it, so that those supplies shall not fail.

In order to do this we must believe in it. Believe in the principle of penitence and open confession which underlies its use.

We must believe with all our heart that no matter how dark may be man's soul, if he will truly repent, there is salvation for him. And equally we must believe that no matter how desirous he may be of better things and how loudly expressive of those desires, unless he truly repents and turns from sin there is no salvation for him.

It is a mistake to overlook the ignorance of many who come to our penitent-forms. Sorrow for sin is no criterion of knowledge of the way of salvation, and penitents must be helped through the mists and struggles of the way to deliverance.

One reason why so many people who apparently get converted don't remain converted is that they did not first explore the ruins of their own heart. You can't build religion on unrepented sins, any more than you can build an enduring house on rubbish or swamp. You must build on a good foundation. Many would-be penitents have such a poor foundation for their religious life that the first storm of temptation brings it down in ruins.

I have no faith in a man's conversion if he is not converted in the old-fashioned Salvation Army way; John Bunyan's way, John Wesley's way, Moody's way, Paul's way, Christ's way, God's way. No man can understand redemption until he understands his own miserable, dark, ruined state. When men are converted in the old-fashioned way they generally stand. In the new-fashioned way they fall.

The Hereditary Principle and the Generalship of The Salvation Army

Commander Evangeline Booth writes on what was a very sensitive matter of Salvation Army policy in 1929 - the selection of succeeding Generals.

From the Staff Review (International Headquarters, London) May, 1929.

The Salvation Army as a Christian Mission among men and women has been at war with sin, by the Grace of God, for sixty-three years. The Army is thus to be reverenced by us who are engaged in its direction not merely as an organization founded, like other organizations, by the will of man, for certain beneficent purposes, but as an integral, authentic and sufficing branch of the holy Church of God in Christ, militant on earth and triumphant in heaven. As a society of sinners saved by the Blood of the Redeemer Himself. For an increasing number of officers and soldiers we offer the only means of grace of which they can avail themselves and the only call to service and sacrifice.

It is the Spirit of God who has led us into the present season of uncertainty. It is a season that has come to us, not through the wisdom of man, not even through any mistakes of which we are conscious, but in fullness of time. At such a season we need to submit ourselves with open minds and due humility to the guidance of our Master alone. It is He who has brought us face to face with the question as to what is His will in respect of our supreme leadership on earth, held by the General and obeyed by us in the name of Christ. There is but one solemn and dominant fact which we need constantly to bear in mind. It is this. Our Lord Jesus Christ and He alone died that we might live. It is He alone who, having died and paid the price, can claim us. Our Army, with its splendid triumphs in the past, its still more splendid victories in the future, is His alone. For His is the Kingdom, the power and the glory, for ever. Amen.

It is the glory of our gospel that it offers the gift of Christ--a full salvation of soul, mind and body--to all nations, men, women and children, whatever their circumstances, rich and poor, learned and ignorant, since all have sinned, and all must perish unless they be saved. If there be any circumstance in our organization which might be liable in the future to limit and thwart the worldwide fulfillment of our divine mission to mankind, now is the time, clearly appointed unto us by the providence of God to adjust it, not in any spirit of controversy or emulation, God forbid, but with a deep sense of what is due from us to the Crucified Redeemer whose we are and whom we serve.

Greatly as the Army has been blessed in its efforts up to the present, we ought not to exclude from our minds and our prayers the possibility that, if we submit ourselves wholeheartedly to the direction of the Almighty, He may be able to use us in the future far above what we can ask or think. Where today we have won thousands for the Savior, tomorrow we may win tens of thousands. Love is power, and there are not limits to the love of God. Arrangements for the conduct of the Army which were wholly suitable and divinely authorized in the day of small things, may be an actual hindrance to the extension of our work and the deepening of our consecration, now that we have been honored by our Lord with a wider call to a far greater service.

No one was more emphatic than our first General (my father honored and revered for all time) in his insistence on the truth that The Salvation Army, in which we are recruited, was founded under Divine inspiration. In the mobilization of that Army it is God's will that this should be alone supreme. That will has been expressed in the truth of Holy Scripture, and the truth of Holy Scripture is fortified by the history of the Christian Church in all ages and all countries.

That our Lord has called apostles for special service and exceptional responsibility is a most evident fact. Such an apostle to the Gentiles was St. Paul (Galatians 2:8). Among the Germans, such an apostle was Martin Luther; among the Scots, John Knox; among the Swiss, John Calvin. In the eighteenth century an apostle of Jesus Christ, John Wesley, worked mightily not only in Old England, but in New England, across the ocean. Gratefully and proudly we acknowledge that, in William Booth, born one hundred years ago, God raised up yet another of His apostles, to be, in Christ, our Founder, not as superseding the Redeemer, but as expressing His love for all men of all nations.

If we study the lives of these apostles, throughout the annals of the Church, we find that in no instance has it ever been the will of God that the office shall be vested in a human family. John Calvin, John Knox and Martin Luther, as reformers, founded no personal dynasty of faith, nor did

George Fox, described as a founder, in Christ, of the Society of Friends. Paul says, "If any other man thinketh that he hath whereof he might trust in the flesh, I more" (Philippians 3:4), but "what things were gain to me, those I counted as loss for Christ (3:7)." I carry a deep and humble pride in my father's lifetime witness for Christ and worldwide service, but even this must be subject to an adoring worship and following to HIS Savior and MINE.

Let us not forget that the hereditary principle, when substituted for God's guidance, led, in the second generation after David, to a division of the Kingdom, solely because of deliberate refusal to listen to the advice or counsel of the elders.

From time to time a son wisely succeeds his father. There was an elder William Pitt and a younger William Pitt, both of them Prime Ministers. The present Archbishop of York is the son of Dr. Temple, who also was a former Archbishop of Canterbury. But the office of Prime Minister is not hereditary, nor is the office of archbishop. In no branch of the Christian Church is there a spiritual authority as absolute as in the Roman Catholic communion. Yet the office of Pope is not hereditary. He is freely elected by the College of Cardinals from among their number.

In the entire range of Christendom, wherever Christ is worshipped, we cannot find one communion, Protestant or Catholic, reformed or unreformed, orthodox or heterodox, vigorous or dying in which the government is held to be associated with a family, however devoted or however saintly. If we examine the records of The Conference on Life and Works, held at Stockholm in 1925, The Conference on Faith and Order, held at Lausanne in 1927, and The Conference on Missions, held at Jerusalem in 1928, at which conferences Christians of all Churches, except the Roman Catholic, met to consider their agreements and disagreements, the hereditary authority in the Church was not so much as mentioned!

In a matter of this importance it is relevant to follow our Lord's method and examine, as He did, the analogies from human experience outside His own faith. The three most impressive founders of religion in the East were Confucius, Buddha and Mohammed. As saviors of the world, we believe they have utterly failed. But they number their disciples by millions. In no case were they able to establish a hereditary headship of their faith. Even in China, where ancestors are worshipped, the family of Confucius exercises no spiritual authority. The case of Mohammed is of particular interest. At his death the question arose whether the leadership of his faith was or was not to be vested in his family. Enough to say that the result was division, developing into numerous schisms and sects.

Turning to temporal sovereignties, we are driven to a similar conclusion. Throughout the world, hereditary autocracies, with unlimited authority, have disappeared altogether, or have been strictly limited and controlled legislatively, judicially and executively, by ministers, councils and parliaments. Even marshals and generals on the battlefield are controlled by prime ministers, war ministers and parliaments.

In Japan there is a constitution. In India the princes are conscious of the change. Europe is largely republican. In Great Britain the kings and queens are honored and beloved because they are advised and supported by a government and a parliament whom the people themselves select. Even in industry the family firm is absorbed in companies where the whole body of proprietors share the duty of electing directors.

Having devoted my whole life to the Army, which has been to me home and children, I am bound to view with anxiety a policy of ignoring and indeed defying what is plainly taught in Scripture, what is plainly to be learned from the Church universal in all ages, what is plainly to be seen in the working of other religious and secular institutions, and what with marked conservative constraint was shown in the framing of the 1904 Supplementary Deed Poll. If today we fail in courage and postpone the adoption of a permanent basis of authority in our Army, we do not escape from the problem. We do not even evade it. An issue which today is urgent, will become not urgent only, but acute.

It is a fact, a serious fact, that at this moment in countries outside the British Empire, The Salvation Army is the only Protestant and evangelical movement which retains an organic union with Great Britain. The Episcopal, or Anglican Church, the Methodists, the Baptists, the Congregationalists, the Presbyterians, the Lutherans and even the Bible Society have every one of them broken away, not in spirit and purpose, but in visible organization. This is true of the United States, and more or less of all nonmissionary countries. The Salvation Army in its union the wide world over stands alone. It is for this glorious unity, organic and spiritual, that I earnestly plead with all the strength at my command. The apparent weakening of this internationalism caused by the acute unrest of the late years has caused me, and I am sure many others, very great distress.

And here let me make my position plain. Whatever red hot fires of criticism, whether by cynics or scientists, are brought to bear on the Gospel of Christ, I would continue to preach that Gospel. It is Christ who saves.

Surely we are ignoring one of the most sacred principles of the word of God if we in any direction or in any way insist upon any procedure that makes it harder for the most humble of our followers to place a wholehearted confidence in the principles of our government: or if we impose upon the chief officers of our organization who are responsible for its advance a system which does not commend itself to the minds of statesmen, financiers and philanthropists as a sound foundation on which to build a government of legislative and educational measures affecting international peoples; a government in which there cannot be found those protective defenses from the evils that have laid low dynasties throughout history.

The teaching of Scripture should once more be our guide. When the fires of Pentecost inspired the earliest Christians, the converts sold their possessions and laid the money down at the apostles' feet (Acts 4:35). That money was sacred. In this advanced age money subscribed for public objects, whether religious or secular, is carefully and rightfully scrutinized, and on one principle, the world over, public opinion is uncompromising. It is this, that in appointments to a trusteeship for public money, no personal influence shall be considered. Even the great foundations established by Rockefeller, Carnegie, Rosenwald, John

Markle and other rich men are managed by trustees wholly independent of kinship by the donors. Yet these donors actually owned in law the money which they gave. They did not collect it, as we collect our funds from the public, and from our own people, the great majority of whom can barely afford to give.

At this point I invite you to follow me with care and to note the precise argument that I wish to put before you. The decision which had to be made does not affect the powers of a duly appointed General. The sole question is how his appointment is to be made. Even should his powers continue to be absolute, that is all the more reason why the manner of his appointment should command the assent of those from whom obedience and devotion are expected.

With the Church of Rome we are bound to disagree on many grave and fundamental matters of faith and practice. But there is one virtue in that Church which we emulate. I refer to the zeal and even the militancy of the Roman Catholic. It is to be attributed, I think, to the fact that a central authority relieves the faithful of many useless questions and sets them free for actual service. It must be so in every army--Salvation Army or other. There must be order. There must be orders given and obeyed. There must be discipline. There must be a central authority, and under present circumstances that authority must be vested in an individual.

But even a Pope, declared by his followers to be infallible, cannot appoint his successor and seldom influences that appointment. At the moment of his death the authority of the Pope reverts at once to the whole

College of Cardinals, who meet in the Sistine Chapel, in secret conclave. After each ballot the voting papers are burned. It is by this method that a great organization has maintained its international character without losing its central authority.

We hold the advantage every way over the Roman Catholic Church. We have a simpler gospel to preach, a more personal Savior as a gift of God to offer. A more glorious salvation by faith alone is emblazoned on our banners. Let us not compromise our opportunity by persisting in arrangements which we have outgrown and by which no church anywhere is impeded.

What I submit for your consideration then is, first: an unrestricted freedom by the High Council to elect the General. How that freedom shall be exercised is a matter not of principle but of method, on which perhaps the High Council itself would wish that the Commissioners of the Army, as at present provided for, should suggest guidance. Let us not be timid. A contested election does no harm. Indeed, it clears the air. For a minority, even if defeated, is much less likely to be disloyal afterwards if it has had a fair chance to express itself. Our rule should be, then, the utmost liberty before election, and the most complete obedience afterwards.

We must not forget that my beloved father, when he founded the Army, was confronted by a "Darkest England." It is his own phrase and, under God, no man did more than he, no man, perhaps, as much, to lighten that darkness. In his efforts he was seconded for many long years by my mother and by my brother Bramwell, the second General of the Army.

But what is the position today? There is still, God knows, a darkness over the lands. But there is also more education. There is also a wider extension of the franchise. There has been in this country, incredible as it would have seemed when the Army was founded, a Labor Government. A measure of constitutional progress within the Army which, thirty years ago, might have been premature, may now be due, and even overdue. Ours is a work of rescue. So may it always be. But we are not now dealing solely with illiterates, with the drunkards, with the wastrels, the prostitutes and the down and outs. Among our leading officers are men and women not only of devotion but of conspicuous ability. Christ Himself has saved them. Christ Himself has called them. His Spirit is working in them and through them. Are we not obligated to make full use of the wisdom which He has bestowed on them and of the abilities which they have surrendered to His service, by demonstrating our confidence in their capacity as well as their loyalty by taking them into our consultation on all matters affecting the work for which they are held responsible? They have a right to be consulted and their loyalty is worthy of our confidence. Such action would immediately result in a tremendous accession of loyalty now held back by the fact that the officers entrusted with the execution of Orders and Regulations have not the smallest voice in the making of them.

In that great charter of the Church (1 Corinthians 12) we read of diversities of gifts, of differences of administration, but "the same spirit" and "the same Lord." It is God who "set some in the church, first apostles, secondarily prophets, thirdly teachers, after that miracles, then gifts of healings, helps, governments, diversities of tongues." It should be our aim to seek these gifts in others, to encourage them, wherever they may be manifest, and by no means to restrict the floodtide of God's grace to any one channel.

The powers of the High Council as defined today by law are limited to the appointment of the General, and when he is appointed it ceases to exist. But I hope, indeed, it is my most earnest prayer, that by the Spirit of God we may have the wisdom to adopt measures, wisely conceived, to obviate any possibility of the recent situation again rising. On that occasion it was owing to an emergency that we were called together. Many of us whose only desire is the good of the Army were placed in a position of apparent--but happily, only apparent--differences of opinion from the view assumed to be held by the retired General.

Speaking as the daughter of my father, the senior representative of his family still on active service in The Salvation Army, I declare to you, with unalterable conviction, that the time has come when the hereditary principle must be brought to an end. It is the duty of the next General to place this office on a broader basis than any kinship, other than a kinship in Christ.

I Only Want the Price of a Small Part of One Battleship

An appeal for the self-denial fund and missionary appeal.

From The War Cry (Chicago) April 9, 1938.

"You are asking for a lot of money for the Self-Denial Effort," said someone to the General the other day.

"Big machines need a lot of fuel!" was the General's instant reply. "I am asking for a lot of money because there is a lot of need. But when I have said all, I am only asking for the price of a small part of one battleship!"

"If you put it like that..." began her questioner. "I do put it like that," broke in the General. "The air is full of the news of rearmament. The nations are getting accustomed to thinking in terms of millions. I read of billions being spent. Governments vote huge sums in order to maintain the object upon which their hearts are set. For the cause upon which the heart of our Savior, the Prince of Peace, is set, I only ask a sum which would buy a little bit of a battleship, or a few tanks, or which would meet the cost of a few hours' modern warfare!

"Do you know," continued the General, "that the product of the whole of the Self-Denial Effort could be put into the breeches of a few guns and blown away in half an hour, the whole result being still further pain and sorrow in the world? Yet, in the crusade of the Prince of Peace, who seeks to heal the brokenhearted and bind up the wounds of humanity, some people dare to say that I ask for a lot of money!"

"It is all a matter of proportion," said her questioner.

"It is all a matter of hard fact!" retorted the General. "Put our highest dreams at a pinnacle beyond the limit of the faith of most of us; lift our total higher than it has ever been--say, as far as $1,500,000 to meet our most urgent mission field needs--and then set that against this annual expenditure, say for example, by Great Britain, where I now live:

On liquor every year	$817,000,000
On tobacco	153,700,000
On confectionery	309,291,000
On motion pictures	508,196,000
On cosmetics	250,000,000
On fireworks	6,451,000

"Fireworks, mind you, a matter of six and one-half million dollars! And you talk about the Army asking for a lot of money!"

"But think of the effort needed to get together what you do ask for, General!"

"I know that we are asking a lot in the way of effort and hours of labor up and down the streets of every city, town and village in this land!" was the warm reply. "I know that the gathering in of the Self-Denial Fund means much sacrifice on the part of the Army's officers, soldiers and friends, but I know also that they are already making the sacrifice with a devotion and eagerness that fills me with legitimate pride and stirs in my heart deepest apprecia-tion and affection for them."

"But the public treats you well, General!"

"I know it! I know that among the public there is enough appreciation of our work to give me the small part of the battleship for which I ask!

"The help that is being given to us means the care of the blind and neglected; it means the keeping alight of the Torch of Love in the darkest corners of the earth; it means the support with material aid of those great pillars of Christlike devotion which have been erected by Salvationists in many lands; it means strengthening the wall against the fear and the godlessness which is sweeping over the world."

"So you don't think you'll ask in vain, General?"

"I believe," was the emphatic reply, "that my small part of one battleship will be furnished by the combined efforts of Salvationists and understanding friends, and I thank them for it!

"In the cause of the Prince of Peace it will accomplish more than the combined navies of the world, no matter how many millions are spent upon them!"

The World's Greatest Romance

The transcript of an address presented in great auditoriums throughout the world. This was recorded by Evangeline Booth, with musical background, and the cassettes are available in various Trade Departments.

The work of The Salvation Army I often describe as the world's greatest romance. This is a bold and startling statement, and may savor of presumption, yet I think as I proceed you will agree that the title is well supported by the story. For, looking through the historic vista of over half a century, we find The Salvation Army a wondrous, chivalrous, adventurous and mysterious tale peculiarly fitting to the term, "romance." But our dictionaries define "romance" as "a most exalted achievement of a most exalted genius." This is just what The Salvation Army is. It is the extremity of an extraordinary imagination made history. The wildest dream of the wildest dreamer materialized. It is the offspring of the greatest love and passion, human and divine, known to the heart of man. Into the fabric of its history is woven heroism of the highest order; miracles of the most convincing character; martyrdom of the truest nature. It is a story throwing into confusion all human probabilities; a story of how God has brought a great thing out of nothing; a story in which He made things which are not to bring to naught things which are, and with His own hand placed the little candle flickering in the darkest places of the earth, high upon a hill, where all the world can see its light.

The Salvation Army is a romance geographically. A ring round a London lamppost expands until it encircles the world.

It is a romance numerically. William and Catherine Booth, my father and mother, sacrificing the promise of a most successful church ministry, start a procession of two along a road in East London with a story to tell, a faith to proclaim. And the procession increases until its train numbers tens of hundreds of thousands.

It is a romance financially. A poverty-stricken mission, begging its bread from door to door to keep its disciples alive, grows into an organization which can appeal to the financial world for the millions necessary to do the work the world is asking it to do.

But, above all, it is a romance spiritually. A young man, our Founder, standing on a slum curb telling the wretched, desolate, churchless masses as they shuffled by in an endless procession, of Jesus Christ, the sinner's Friend, becomes a leader of an army of hosts of men and women who cry in all the languages of the earth, "Behold the Lamb of God who taketh away the sin of the world."

So, perhaps it is not too much to say that The Salvation Army is the world's greatest romance.

The birth of The Salvation Army was a romance. This organization was not born amidst hushed and sacred influences. This organization was born amid the roaring thunder of the darkest neighborhood of the great metropolis-- London--under a murky sky in choking fog and spattering rain--the shrill call of the street hawker--the cries of pitiful little children--the coarse laughter of the girl of the street--the curses and oaths of drunken brawlers. It was born in lodging houses, damp cellars, blind alleyways, fever stricken courtyards, the deep recesses of the great bridge, where ragged forms staggered into darkness and fair faces vanished for the last time. It was born where wickedness is without restraint and poverty reaches the lowest stratum of human want. Born amid indescribable horrors, the unmasterful miseries, the inestimable sorrows, sins and tragedies of the underworld. It was born like our Lord and Savior, an outcast by the wayside. It was born like Bethlehem's meteor, a flash, a star in a midnight sky.

Do you know what I think? I think it was a miracle for all time how this thought of God for the churchless masses dropped into the heart of a man. It is a story for all eternity how the great oak, now spreading its branches under every sky for the shelter of the poor of every nation, is a little seedling dropped in a London street gutter.

The Salvation Army's ministry of the streets is a romance. I sometimes think that even those who know us best overlook the service we render the nations in our ceaseless warfare against all that is evil and our maintained advocacy of all that is good in the open street. With unflinching courage we denounce any and every influence that is opposed to the nation's good. We seek to inspire the poor and the ignorant--the highest form of patriotism. I say the highest because we are ever preaching righteousness and it is righteousness that exalteth a nation. It is the principle of righteousness upon which, alone, just and correct government can stand. A nation is great and will increase in greatness only in proportion to the way her people, in precept and in practice, individually and nationally, adhere to the God-inspired principles of truth. Does not the writing upon the wall of our suffering world today tell us that a nation's forces are not alone in the strength of its fleets, the size of its armies, the wealth of its treasury, the extent of its territories, the power of its air force, or even the wisdom of its politics? A nation's power is rather to be found in its world influences. Its ascendancy is righteousness, in the authority of its enlightened teaching--these are the forces which give to a people predominance among the nations of the earth. And so, the officers of The Salvation Army stand in the street--in the frost, in the fog, in the rain and in the sun--and, in the simple language of the common people, tell of God's wondrous love to man.

Brook Dan was the name the mountain town had given him when he left his Australian home to seek gold in America with his newlywed wife, whose hair the sun had kissed and into whose eyes two stars had fallen. The neighbors said they never did see such a handsome pair--Dan, six foot in his stocking feet, broad of shoulder, brave of spirit, kindly of face, the coach of his varsity football team and the stroke of his varsity crew.

Do you know how a man falls or loses his footing at the edge of a precipice? This is how Brook Dan fell into an abyss of darkness and sin when he mingled with the godless crowd of the gold seekers.

Then, one night, Brook Dan, coming up the mountain trail, broken in hope, in heart, in life, heard singing. Yes, it was singing, singing in the open street! There was music, too. Good music. It seemed to come with the snow, and the snow seemed to have no thought but to make everybody white. Memories, as a great surge, swept over his soul. He saw himself, seven years of age, dressed one hour too soon that he might be in time at the church to hear the organist play. He saw himself at 18 years of age, taking the organist's place, and his mother's eyes, all smiles, looking up at him. He looked down at his shoes. They did not cover his feet. His coat was in rags. His hat? He had lost it somewhere.

Then, thoughts of Dad. Dad, so proud of him. Dad, who said, "Come home to us strong and good and brave." He crept up behind the bandsmen and stood on the outskirts of the street meeting. No one would see him. But the man they called Captain did see him, and slipped his arm around his shoulder, saying, "Pray, Dan, pray." And they kept on singing..."but that Thy blood was shed for me."

A woman ran and told his wife that her husband was praying, and all the way down the mountain trail she ran, her golden hair blowing in the wind and the baby in her arms. And with broken voice and outstretched arms, Dan asked, "If God forgives me, can you?" and, turning to the bandsmen, he cried, "Boys, if there's a prayer left in your heart, pray for me!" The Captain placed the drum in the center of the ring and, Dan and his wife kneeling there, joined in the hymn, "O Lamb of God, I come." And the snow came down and made the penitents white.

Dan became the bandmaster of the corps, and his exemplary life, coupled with his exceptional talents, gave him a place on the Board of Councilmen. Twelve years after, the mayor gave the city a public holiday when he passed away, which made it possible for crowds to gather around his grave and carry out his dying request to sing the hymn that brought about his salvation.

The story of Salvation Army bands is a romance. I think I can speak of Salvation Army bands as one having authority. On many occasions, I have been called to lead the battle for the right to play brass instruments on the streets, when sorely opposed by local authorities and the populace. Now, we who have thought about music have discovered that the secret of its marvelous influence is its quick appeal to the human heart. The relation of music is not to ideas, but to the emotions. Music does not first sound the depth of knowledge, it first sounds the depth of feeling. It does not excite to argument or criticism. It awakens a yearning to listen, to receive and to follow. The strains of a country's national hymn do not offer an elaborate definition of patriotism, but they quicken the heartbeat of every patriot to deeds of desperate daring in defense of his country's liberty. It did not take my father long to discover that even beneath tattered garments there is love of harmony; that music appeals to the lowly and uneducated as readily as to the high and tutored.

The cornet and the drum are among the earliest vehicles to attract the masses. At first, they met with bitter opposition and our people were beaten with sticks and stones. Many of them were imprisoned for more than a month at a time. Yet, the progress of our musical forces was so rapid that now there is not an instrument of wind, of key, of pipe, of reed, of string, of parchment, of brass, of wood, of steel or of bone that has not been marshalled into the ministry of The Salvation Army. We have carried spiritual and patriotic music to the congested byways, to the prison cells and to the places of congregated vice and misery.

Attracted by the shining brass, the quick march and the well-known hymn, drunkards have left their drink, girls have come out of their haunts of iniquity, mothers have forsaken their places of toil and little children have turned from their play. The ne'er-do-wells, the loafers, the dull of conscience and the broken of spirit, indeed, the well dressed, who have pursued evil and forgotten good, have followed on the sidewalks to keep within hearing of the strains lifted by over 130,000 senior and junior Salvation Army musicians in every part of the world--some marching under scorching suns of tropical countries and some under arctic skies of northern lands--who give their musically trained service without payment of any kind.

Also, our musicians have taken the inspiring influences of sacred song to the desolate and the cheerless. Many of the bedridden poor, languishing in tenement basements, have caught the strains of the old hymn, "Abide with me from morn till eve, for without Thee, I cannot live. Abide with me when night is nigh, for without Thee, without Thee, I dare not die."

Yes, The Salvation Army has maintained an unbroken note of love, help and peace the whole world over.

The history of Salvation Army literature is a romance. Theodore Roosevelt said, "Who can estimate The Salvation Army's contribution to the world's good in the output of its evangelistic printing presses?"

We started with *The War Cry*. Small--700 a week. But now, 131 different periodicals printed in over 73 languages, not including many dialects, confronting four-fifths of the human race in their own tongue, with an aggregate circulation of four million per issue, have, as white winged messages of happiness, help and hope, enriched the world. Not one inch of our *War Cry* is given to commercial advertisement. Its every word is concentrated upon and consecrated to the uplift and salvation of men. It is an intrepid, unflinching declaration of the old truths, the unalterable, imperishable Gospel of Jesus Christ and, in this day of destructive criticism, the pernicious and seductive teaching of dissection and contradistinction of the Bible, in this day of infidel attack upon the fundamental truths of Christianity, snatching the prop of eternal hope from old age as it stands with one foot in the damp sod of the grave, and robbing youth of its one unerring lamp as it starts down the snare-strewn path of life, in this day of unlimited batterings upon the Christ of the Cross, this *War Cry*, this humble little newspaper with its immortal lettering outstrides the storm and goes forth a tongue of fire supporting the story of the Babe of Bethlehem, defending the impregnable and everlasting standards of the Bible and championing the sacrifice of the Lamb of God, dying on Calvary for a world's transgression.

You will find this *War Cry* everywhere. In the palaces of the rulers of nations and thrown on the bunks of lumbermen's shanties. You will find it in the rich man's mansion and in the toiler's home. You will find it in the business office of large affairs and tucked under the fruit of the pushcart. You will find it laid under picturesque droplights in fashionable libraries and held up to poor eyesight by trembling hands in the almshouse. You will find it wet with the salty spray on the whaling smack off Labrador. You will find it thumbed by black fingers in the Hottentot's hut and the Zulu's kraal. You will find it spelled over by the leper's dimmed eyes amid the exotic fragrance of southern isles. You will find it dispelling the weariness of the bullock-cart traveler as he journeys over India's scorched sands. You will find it gladdening the heart of the lonely flax-gatherer in the desolate island of St. Helena. You will find it the only piece of literature in the city slum. You will find it held up by condemned hands to catch the sunshine that filters through prison bars. You will find it sounding the same note, singing the same song, carrying the same hope, telling the same story that has echoed the ages, imperishable in its truth, unalterable in its efficacy, everlasting in its glory, the Gospel of Jesus Christ, the power of God unto salvation.

It is a romance, how the Army has spread. The Founder did not have at his disposal trained men and women to start The Salvation Army. He did not have ordained ministers, or even men trained in the tactics of his own warfare. In many lands, the government and the populace were against us, and frontiers were guarded to prevent our entrance. Yet, as a vibrating, pulsating electric current, The Salvation Army got across the English Channel, left the railroad tracks, swept the sea and girdled the world

This is just an example of how it happened: two red Indians leave Port Essington in northwestern America in their birchbark canoe. They land at Vancouver, Canada, their loins girded with the skins of wild beasts of their forests, feathers standing up from their hair. On their high cheekbones (is) painted the scarlet emblem of their tribe; one of them, totally blind.

And at an Army street meeting on that dark night, under that dark sky, those two dark souls found the Light of the World, Jesus. On their return trip, no boat ever carried a more precious cargo, a Salvation Army song book wrapped in a piece of deerskin, tucked under the seat of the birchbark canoe. With what result? All along the receiving sands of the western ocean you will find a red man in his great tabernacle of the mighty forest, or upon the heights of some deserted, windswept plateau, lifting his prayers no more to an incomprehensible mystery, but to an all-comprehended God. And you will hear him as I did, in the white night of the far North, three or four hundred, their dusky countenances illuminated with the down-flashing of revelation. And you will hear them singing, "At the Cross, at the Cross, where I first saw the light."

It is a romance how two men, not ordained ministers, a milkman and a bricklayer, started The Salvation Army in Australia, the land of the Southern Cross. And today its hills echo and reecho with the music of Salvation Army bands, and its plains are made picturesque with the red and blue of Salvation Army uniforms worn by outstanding exemplars of all for which your Blood and Fire flag is the imperishable emblem.

No church dignitary started The Salvation Army in Canada. It was not even a commissioned officer of the Army. It was a simple soldier raising the Blood and Fire flag in the streets of Toronto. But in the cities of that great dominion and across its vast plains, in town and hamlet, you will see the red and blue of the Salvation Army uniform.

How was The Salvation Army started in the United States? I did not start it. No ordained minister started it. A little girl, sixteen years of age, from the cotton mills of Manchester, England, passing a broken down stable in Philadelphia, the birthplace of the Republic, said, "Oh, Mother! What a lovely place to start the work of The Salvation Army--like Jesus, born in a stable!" And, as from that stable in Bethlehem thousands of years ago have come all the bells of salvation that are ringing around the world, so from that stable in Philadelphia have come the ten thousand activities of The Salvation Army in this country for helping the poor, for reclaiming the sinner, for looking after and cheering old age, for educating and training the underprivileged boy, for converting the convict into an honorable citizen, for taking the little children of the slums to our fresh air camps, for all the love and new hope that goes to that class of whom the world speaks only in a whisper, those who have lost their way and know not where to turn for help.

Like the girl, so fair, so young, who, with eyes wide and throbbing heart, listens to his promises. Why, they were wonderful! They would have a sweet little home together and he would always take care of her! So, with her hand cold and nervous locked in his strong, feverish fingers, they slipped out upon the highway that led to the great city. She would see life! But as they passed the grand old church at midnight, the pavement, black in the spattering rain, did not look to her like the way of life. She thought it looked like the way of death, and shuddered. Then, the little lowdown lodging-house, then the promise to marry her the next morning, then the startled awakening, calling his name at dawn and getting no answer, then her inability to understand the lodging-house woman when she kept repeating, "He left early. He said he would not be back and paid for the night's lodging."

Then the shattering blow of the realization that the promises he made were all bubbles and that she was an outcast. Then, Mother--poor Mother!-- she would be looking for her. Looking everywhere. Father will be saying she should never be let in the house again like he did about that other man's daughter who ran away. Then, a knocking on the door. Then, her own voice that seemed to be coming from away off while her heartbeat hammered in her throat: "Who are you? You cannot come in!" Then, a voice. The voice that called her in from the garden when she was only two years of age. The voice said, "Kitty, it is Mother. I have come to take you home. Father is outside in the taxi anxiously waiting for you. Come, little Kitty. Come home."

The story is, the lodging-house keeper had a heart. When she observed the soul agony and the young eyes, she said, "I'm going to that Salvation Army woman. She will know just what to do with a case like this. Why, she's only a little kid." And the girl's mother, after the search for Kitty grew fruitless, through sobs and tears said, "I'm not going to say a word to the police. I shall tell that Salvation Army woman. She will find her if anybody can!"

And that Salvation Army officer was the very same woman that the lodging-house keeper had contacted. Oh, this Salvation Army! This beautiful Salvation Army with its ability to love, to serve and to save!

You ask, "What is the secret of all this achievement for the world's good? From whence its power?" The power is our faith. Our faith in the gospel we preach. We believe what we preach and we preach what we believe. We preach God is Creator of heaven and earth, omnipotent and unerring. The help of the helpless. The hope of the hopeless. The champion and protector of the defenseless. We preach God, the Son, the world's Redeemer, saving the worst of men.

We preach that the most degraded wretch crawling out of the ditch of his abominations, if he will but cry unto God for mercy, will find Him, an all-pardoning Redeemer. We preach the Holy Ghost, Comforter and Sanctifier of the souls of men, holding up the human heart under life's distresses and kindling lights in its shadowed places.

We preach grace. Grace enough, grace enough for you and for me, for life and for death. We preach the Bible--the Word of God--the one unalterable standard of everlasting right and everlasting wrong. Authentic in its statements. Immaculate in its teaching. All solemn in its judgments and glorious in its promises.

We preach hell. The soul's suicide, the eternal punishment of the persistent and willful rejector of Jesus Christ.

We preach heaven, the eternal home of our loved ones gone before; the reward of the good.

We preach for all men, whether under Californian skies or on Siberian salt fields. We preach it in song, we teach it in word and in deed. We preach it to the white, to the black, to the red, to the bronze and to the yellow. The eternal gospel! The inestimable, fathomless, boundless, measureless ocean of God's love!

Do you know what I believe? I believe the rocks will turn grey with age. The forests will become unmoored in the hurricane. The sun will shut its fiery eyelid. The stars will drop like burned out ashes. The hills will stagger and go over. The seas will heave their last expiring groan. The world will wrap itself in sheets of flame. But God's love will never die. It will kindle new suns when all other lights have gone out. It will be an ever-billowing ocean when all other waters have swept themselves away. It will sing while the archangel's trumpet peals amid the crash of toppling sepulchers and the rush of the wings of the rising dead!

This is the world's greatest romance: GOD'S LOVE!

* * * * *

Our Founder's Last Dream

Notes of an address delivered at the opening of the Eastern Territorial Memorial Training College.

From The War Cry (New York) August 19, 1922.

My father's dreams--some day when the War's importunities clamor with less insistence and my pen has pace to run and my heart to outpour upon such a theme, I am going to write about our Founder's dreams and what they have meant to the world.

All those whose names fame's chisel has inscribed upon the tables of time as leaders of men--prophet or patriot, statesman or saint, merchant prince or humanitarian--have been dreamers of dreams--men of vision. With the eye of genius they have wrestled and wrought until the ideal born and nurtured in their own heart took substance and stood revealed in concrete form before the eyes of men.

So did my father's vision enrich a world. The fulfillment of his dreams encircles the globe, memorializing his inspired personality wherever the institutions of Blood-and-Fire altruism are to be found.

Unconventional and Unworldly

My father dreamed of a crusade extraordinary against the legions of iniquity--a crusade unconventional, unostentatious, unworldly, asking unprecedented sacrifices on the part of its followers in the interest of the immortal soul. From this one man's vision The Salvation Army sprang, its small and obscure beginnings giving little foreshadow of the mighty instrument of God it was destined to become, perpetuating the life-passion of its author among all people.

My father dreamed a troubled dream of the wrongs and wrecks submerged by modern civilization and, mirrored in the glass of inspiration, he saw strong arms outstretched, lifeboats riding the wave and, a myriad salvage apparata at work for the rescue of human derelicts.

Thus were born the innumerable philanthropies of the Army's social wing, which has opened vistas of possibility for the reformation, rehabilitation and regeneration of the pariah of society and, along which broken humanity has passed to newness of life, while outside this organization's immediate sphere it has blazed the trail for countless settlements of social welfare instituted by other denominations, for all which our hearts overflow with gratitude to God and afresh praise Him for our Founder.

Full Years and Experience

Once again my father dreamed. This time "the Apostle of the Poor" was nearing the end of his long pilgrimage, full of years and experience. His travels had taken him into every center of the civilized world, his phenomenal lifework had brought him recognition from kings, bishops, statesmen, magnates in every walk of civic, national and ecclesiastical life. He had prayed in the chambers of congress, he had addressed Parliaments in session, he had been received with honor by the world's foremost seats of learning, one of the oldest of which had conferred on him the degree of Doctor of Civil Laws. In these professional circles and influential atmospheres the soul of my father was moved to dream again--that Calvary-lit soul which had thought and felt since boyhood selflessly and supremely for the souls of others. He coveted for his people the advantages of education, mental preparedness, physical fitness and knowledge which alone could equip them for the unequal task in the salvation of mankind.

So my father dreamed of a University of Humanity--a chain of Colleges belting the world--the curriculum of which should have as its sole design the teaching and training of "saviors of men." Existing universities provided for every science but the science of humanity, a subject so separate and distinct that it called for the setting apart of schools of learning, as it has always demanded the setting apart of the lives of its students. The General's wisdom took cognizance of the difficulties, dangers and unforeseen situations awaiting the man who makes the amelioration of mankind his chosen profession, and he planned educational institutions which should specialize in that branch of learning which would at once arm and outfit a servant of God and mankind. These institutions were intended not to do away with the Army Training Colleges already in existence, but to amplify and consolidate their spheres of usefulness which, while excellent in themselves, were wholly inadequate in view of the transcending need.

This was my father's last dream, outlined to the world in his University scheme--a precious legacy not only because it defined one of the dearest visions of my father's heart, but because it was one of the very few of which we failed to see the fulfillment. Some of the finest minds in the Eastern and Western worlds eulogized the masterly proposal, some funds were subscribed, but for various reasons the actual establishment of the great project was deferred. Like prophecy now read the General's own words, penned in some scheme: "If not in my time, then in the days of those who will fill my position and take up my work after I have reached my Home on High. I verily believe this undertaking to be of God, and sooner or later it must and will be carried on. Someone, somewhere, some day will have the honor and win the reward of furnishing the means for the establishment of our worldwide, world helping University of Humanity."

Perpetuate Ruling Passion

Shafts of bronze and obelisks of stone could never adequately memorialize the Army's first General! Millions of his spiritual children felt as one that his monument must be something vital, enduring, beneficent--something that should not only commemorate but perpetuate the ruling passion of their Founder's life, that should provide, indeed, an increasing reproduction of lives akin in purpose and spirit to that of the great Founder himself. In these monuments there has come the realization of his vision, for in many lands there are being dedicated spacious and commodious institutions to be known as Memorial Colleges, in which the scheme he conceived and cherished can be put into practical effect.

My father's interest in the undertaking, as it concerned the United States, was, I know, exceptional. He esteemed New York as a mighty pivot and, hoped here to establish the parent University of the Western hemisphere. He realized the tremendous influence which all America gives to education and specialization, and he repeatedly told me that for such training, undertaken with American vim of spirit and alertness of mentality for the benefit of consecrated young Americans, with all their essential characteristics of "go, grit and gumption," the possibilities were beyond anything ever produced in any theological or sociological school the world over.

Joy and Satisfaction

Remembering all this, it may be understood when I say that in announcing the opening of the Memorial Training College in New York on April 10, the anniversary of my father's birth, I experience a thrill of personal joy and satisfaction such as not been mine since God called my father Home.

There was just one aspect of the undertaking which the General did not foresee. He hoped and desired that the finances of the scheme should come from the wealthy few rather than from the small exchequers of the working classes. As a matter of fact, the funds for the memorial Training College in America have come from both classes and have been supplemented in a large measure by the voluntary subscriptions of my officers themselves, who with great hearts, though small purses, have denied themselves to help toward this happy consummation of the General's last scheme.

This latter fact has great significance, for who better than they could adequately estimate the mental, spiritual and physical drain of such work and understand how imperatively necessary it is that such fitness be given to all who first stand in the front line of this battlefield? These officers gave themselves; now they have given that others may have double to bestow upon the mightiest task on earth--the effectual ministering to the needy world and the saving of the lost.

New Era in Education

With the launching of the undertaking a new era opens in sociological, religious and philanthropic education, the far reaching issues of which only ages yet to come will reveal. We know that as today the world's men of mark look back with affection to the particular alma mater of their student days, and those famous colleges inscribe upon their honor roll names of the great of all nations, so in the years to be will leaders in religious and social redemption recall with gratitude their graduation from the University of Humanity, which will in turn cherish the names of those whom it will send forth girded with strength, fortified with wisdom and baptized with divine unction to turn many to righteousness and to shine as the stars forever and ever.

The Storm

In 1896, at the age of thirty, Eva was appointed to America to heal the breach in the ranks caused by the defection of Maude and Ballington Booth. From scores of papers from this period of crisis, we present the following:

A. *The letter which she sent to American officers upon her arrival in New York.*

My Dear Comrade:

Now that the General has appointed me to the command of the United States until the arrival of the new Commissioners, I hasten to place myself in your hands in this season of deep and heartrending sorrow, to be of what service God can enable me to push forward the salvation of souls.

It has given me untold comfort in this terrible storm to receive assurances of loyalty from the Brigadiers, Divisional and Field Staff. Every hour brings me from all parts of the field testimonies of the sorrow felt on the one hand and unswerving loyalty on the other. I will therefore confine my first letter to you to expressing a few heartfelt feelings suggested by the circumstances of the hour:

1. Do not be influenced to a final decision on the whole case until the General's return to England, when he

has promised to fully consider and decide upon the issues involved.

2. Remember, that heavy and bitter as is the blow that has fallen upon you, which I fain would have shielded you from, had it been possible, it cannot be as painful as for those of his own family, who would gladly have laid down their lives to avert the disaster.

3. Let me ask you to fix your minds upon the principles at stake. Should the General make one law for America and another for India--apply one law to his son and another to his Brigadiers and Field Officers? These questions lie at the root of the present distress, and it is to preserve the unity of the whole Army that the General has felt it right to decide and act as he has done.

4. Be true to your pledges. The gaze of the whole world is fixed upon America, and especially on its officers, at this hour. I believe in you. I believe it because of your past faithfulness and devotion, because of struggles through which you have fought and because of the

victories won for the cause in the past and because you know the power as well as the grace of obedience.

5. Stand by the Army. It is worldwide in its unity, benevolence and purpose.

6. Be careful to avoid encouraging any party or personal feeling. Cultivate the gift of love, speak evil of and think evil of no one.

7. Have faith in God! We shall overcome. But we can only do so by fighting in the confidence that our principles are divine.

8. Give me your trust. I am alone. My heart is broken. This command has been suddenly and unexpectedly given me. I feel my responsibility, and I want to bless you and help you and guide you.

9. Pray for me. Write me concerning your sorrow. I am a sharer of it, and with what consolation I receive I shall give, and I am sure I need not ask you to continually remember before the Throne our beloved

> General--the father of our movement. His spirit will be torn--his heart lacerated. Our prayers and love must sustain him.

I pray that the God of all grace and peace will fill you with consolation, and the power of the Holy Ghost give you courage and desperate faith, and while the waters of this grief beat rudely around us, unity shall be our strength, while we stand 'neath the shadow of the Cross and the wave of the Salvation Army flag.

Rely upon me as your sister and comrade in this holy war for God, America and the world.

EVA C. BOOTH,
COMMISSIONER

B. *Quotations from her address in London upon her return to International Headquarters five months later.*

From The War Cry (Toronto) June 13, 1896.

When Miss Booth rose to speak, everyone stood up, and it was some moments before the applause permitted of her voice being heard. For an hour she spoke with divine inspiration, a torrent of eloquence and a touching depth of feeling.

During the course of her address, Miss Booth spoke most highly of her brother Herbert (our Commandant).

The mention of the Commandant's name evoked prolonged applause.

* * * * *

Said the Commissioner: Nations were intent upon seeing how the Salvationists would weather the storm. What did they see? Loyal men, whose hearts were torn, and courageous women, with anguished breasts, still marching on unflinchingly. Some of them wrote on at their office desks, while others stood, perhaps alone, at distant corps. Nobly the hosts have stood the shock, with scarcely a regrettable exception, from the highest Staff officer to the trembling, frightened little Junior.

The soldiers! Oh, how I love them! Yes, I have always loved our rank and file, but these months in America have taught me to love them as never before. Many of them have served in our ranks until their hair has turned from bronzy brown to dusky grey, and from them there have poured into Headquarters scores of such wires as "God and The Salvation Army till death," "Loyalty to the Flag," etc.

And again: "Truly I realized that I was the least of my Father's house when the wire came, ordering me to jump to the bridge. For five nights and days I had neither slept nor had my coat off my back, and food had scarcely passed my lips." In that day God Himself drew near and fought for us. To my soul He gave the words: "In this thy day," and over me swept the realization that to me had been given an opportunity such as has rarely been offered a warrior of the Cross since the days of the early martyrs. To me was granted the privilege of strengthening hearts passing through the sorest test of a lifetime; of healing broken hearts; and of being a little candlelight in a midnight of blackest despair.

It was my day to prove to my God, to those gazing o'er heaven's battlements, to the grinning fiends in hell, to my own soul, to my General and father, that I was willing to fling my whole being into the ghastly breach; yea, it was my day to minister unto the Lord's own loved ones, who in bitterest sorrow, darkest mystery and sorest temptation, were, with bleeding spirits, pressing on the War.

Miss Booth concluded by saying: The time is flying, and I have not said all I should of Colonel Nicol's unflagging zeal and of Commissioner Carleton's wise counsels. And now you must go on to pray for the Consul (cheers), and Commissioner Booth-Tucker. They have a hard, hard fight ahead, but we know them to be God-sustained warriors.

Chapter Six

Music and Musicians

How Music Helps The Salvation Army

Quoted in The War Cry (Toronto) of December 8 and 15, 1990. Originally published in Etude Magazine in 1944.

My father said, "The Salvation Army makes constant use of music." Music belongs to God. It is of God and was created by Him. Man realizes that something more than the material is in him, and this he expresses in music. Is there any other influence that carries the power of music and song? Music, you see, is the quickest educator in the world. It is the master of order, time, courteous obeisance; it expands the poorest mental understanding: it makes people milder, kinder. It gives birth to highest aspiration and kills the ignoble with one blow of melody. And so our organization utilizes the all-conquering influence of music to break down what is evil and build up what is good. I have known a murderer in his cell to resist every word I spoke, but when, taking up my guitar, I sang to him, "Just as I am without one plea, but that Thy Blood was shed for me," he burst into tears and asked me to pray.

Music creates conviction; more than that, it reveals the compassion of God.

Symphony--a consonance of sounds, and sympathy--a consonance of feelings, are inseparably allied. You must have feeling in music or it is lifeless; you must have harmony in feeling or there is discord. What is war but the bitter fruit of inharmonious feelings? Every composition springs from a specific purpose in the composer's heart: our music springs from an exhaustless thirst to bring knowledge of the Savior to the hearts of men. The first thing a converted man wants to do is to sing.

Thus, there is a philosophy behind our use of music. When the Greeks built the city of Thebes they had music played, and it so inspired them that the stones seemed to move into place of themselves. We are trying to build a better world, and we find that the music of reverence, of comfort, of repentance teaches faith and gives birth to the noblest aspirations.

Our street music, of trumpets and tambourines, is meant not merely to attract attention. Attracting attention is important to any great enterprise, but the chief concern is what you attract that attention from and what you attract it to. Our use of music is to attract attention away from worldly thoughts and attract it to the spiritual. As a girl, I would sing in the worst saloons of London, accompanying myself on the accordion, and many of the men would stop drinking and sing with me.

Street music, however, by no means represents the whole of our musical work. Music forms an important part in our training of officers. In all our training schools, voice culture, instruments, harmony and composition are taught by thoroughly equipped musicians, all of them Salvationists. Many belong to families who have been Salvationists for three generations, inheriting the tradition of our music, as part of the warm atmosphere of home. And what is this tradition? To do good is the purpose of every note we sound. Thus, the Army is bright in its music. By no means neglecting the music of pathos, we try to make people glad.

Our music is kept simple and pure, and the plain people take it with them into their workshops and their kitchens. All our textbooks and all the selections in our band journals (over 2,000 arrangements) are written by Salvationists. Our bandsmen number nearly 60,000 and our songsters, over 80,000. The world's greatest artists--among them Sousa, Sir Thomas Beecham and Kreisler--have encouraged us by their congratulations. Yet our music has not been evoked by wealth or endowment. Our bandsmen receive not one cent of remuneration for all the time and toil they give, early and late, on work days and rest days, under all skies, Arctic and tropical. Repeatedly, the quality of their work earns them calls from well-playing professional groups; yet they always reject these tempting monetary offers from the outside. Their sacrificial service springs from their knowledge of the power of music to appeal to hearts.

More than any other art, music is appreciated by the uneducated, for almost everyone has an acute sense of the beauty of melody and harmony. Music was never meant for the educated alone; its most direct appeal is not to ideas but to human emotions. Music does not incite to argument or even to a desire for learning; it awakens a desire to receive, to follow, to obey. The strains of a country's national hymn do not offer an elaborate definition of patriotism--but they quicken the heartbeat of every patriot to deeds of daring.

The harp, which I dearly love, is among the most ancient achievements of civilization. Excavations in the Mesopotamian Valley brought to light the frame of a harp. On the harp there is the closest contact between the human hand and the source of the tone, without intervening mechanism. Thus the harp is an intimate expression of personality. That, perhaps, is why in the beatific vision of heaven, harps are played.

It is not merely with the appreciation of music, however, that we of The Salvation Army are concerned. We aim at nothing less than musical creation. All over the world, Army brigades have made silent people sing. I can never forget an experience in India. It was a dark night; no moon, no stars. The heavens were one black stretch. My train, late, did not reach its destination until two in the morning. On stepping to the platform, I heard a simple melody of my own composition carried on sweetest silver notes. "This is the boys' flute band, 50 of them," said the Commissioner. "They are all the sons of redeemed criminals. Their instruments are made by their own hands, from the 'reeds' of their fields. They are such good boys! I don't know how we could get on without them!" I thought of their fathers, once criminals in chains but now redeemed, and remembered the bruised reed which He shall not break!

A week or so later, I stood in one of our Army leper colonies, some of the patients lying before me on stretchers. My tears would keep coming, and in my soul I prayed God's pardon for the smallness of my faith while those smitten with the terrible scourge sang,

> "Jesus, Thou art everything to me;
> All my lasting joys are found in Thee."

Then, in simplest language, I explained what it means for Jesus to be everything, and their large, pensive eyes took on the light of spiritual understanding. Dr. Noble, our commanding officer, said, "We do very little preaching here. We sing."

Melody is memory. Some time ago, in a war-torn part of the world, the enemy came to annihilate a village. The Salvation Army crowded the Sabbath-school hall with children, as a place of refuge. On hearing the ominous tread of the approaching troops, the officer said, "Sing--sing as loud as you can!" The little ones began to sing, "Jesus loves me, this I know." As they reached the line, "They are weak but He is strong," the enemy leader entered the hall. With tears blinding his eyes and his hands full of money, he said, "Here, take this and buy them something to eat. I sang that song when I was a little boy."

From its very inception, The Salvation Army has sensed the love of harmony in even the most discordant hearts. Throughout the world into the shadowed places where men are lashed by the rods of their own folly, our bands have carried the uplifting influences of Miriam's tambourines, Gideon's trumpets, David's songs. We know that music is a supreme blessing, a communion between self and what is beyond all self.

A musician who composes to excite evil does a great disservice to society. There have always been sounds (termed music) that degrade people. Some composers do not hesitate to use music for the expression not of the "spirituals" of a great race, but of the barbaric surge of primeval passion--the scream of cacophonous discord. I need not specify such so-called music further than that. We of The Salvation Army hold that the Supreme Being is a harmony within Himself, and it follows that faith in the Divine must evoke a corresponding spirit of harmony.

Salvation is a miracle, but it is not a conjuring trick or an illusion. It is a deliberate process and, we have found, a successful recovery of lost values in men, women and even children. Everything that encourages the good in man is an ally of salvation. Music, at its best and noblest, has always been an ally of The Salvation Army. At our Lord's Last Supper they sang a hymn. He who was about to be crucified joined in that hymn. From that day on, the Church has been a singing comradeship.

We talk a great deal about art for art's sake. We in The Salvation Army believe that music is for man's sake. A great virtuoso is as much the servant of man as a great physician. He was not endowed with his genius merely in order to exhibit acrobatic skill on an instrument. He was called to be a leader in the infinities of meaning beyond the range of words. In The Salvation Army we sometimes tell rich people that their money is not their own. We tell beautiful people that their fascination is not their own. It is a channel, opened by God, to attract the souls of men to Himself.

To My Bandsmen

A challenge in two parts.

From The War Cry (New York) November 5 and 12, 1927.

Music has been well said to be the speech of angels. It is universal in its appeal. There is not an ear it cannot attract, not a heart it cannot melt. The high and low, educated and ignorant, glad and sad, good and bad, are all fascinated and held by the power of music. It voices aspirations and shapes the destinies of peoples. An ancient sage wisely said that if he were allowed to make the songs of a nation, he would not care who made its laws.

The great Creator, in His infinite outpouring of blessings, has given to every human creature an innate sense of harmony to which, although he may not be able to produce it, he responds in some form or other. Perhaps the appeal comes from art, or poetry, or oratory, or it may be from the frozen music of architecture. But almost universally man is attracted by it and answers quickly to its melodious challenge.

The Maker of all things purposed this when He filled the world with harmony. Upon the vine-strung branches of the forest the winds harp it; the oceans, as colossal organs, peal it; and the reverberating drums of the thunders echo. Feathery-throated songsters sing it--even in the green grass, the dry and scorched sands, the ploughed, upturned sod, the ant-hillock, there are millions of twitterings and murmurings of creatures uniting in one Hallelujah of praise.

What heart can remain unmoved in the country on a Summer morn? The trumpeters of light, advancing from eastern skies, heralding a newborn day! Nature's diapason pealing. The most insignificant flower is beautified. The verdure of the hills carries a mystic sheen. The lily blooming on the face of silent waters is glorified. Music in sky, music on earth, music everywhere; music feathered and scaled, hoofed and horned and winged. The bees hum it, the frogs croak it, the squirrel chatters it, the woodpecker taps it, the quail whistles it, the lark carols it, the swallows call it, the lamb bleats it, the cattle low it--music up on the mountain, in the valley, across the plain; music on the waters, happy, glad, glorious.

"Even in the mud and scum of things,
Something sings, sings, sings!"

Throughout the Holy Scriptures, from Genesis to Revelation, we find references to music, both instrumental and vocal--from the creation of the first songbird to St. John's inspired description of the music and singing of the Heavenly City.

We read of Miriam and her Hebrew women celebrating with song and timbrel the crossing of the Red Sea! Gideon and his followers with trumpets routing the enemy; David, whose songs have come down through the ages, filling earth and sky with exaltation and praise to the Holiest in the Height; the great choir of 245 appointed by the Jews to celebrate their return from captivity in Babylon.

Then the Bible speaks of the sweetest song that ever ascended to the Father's Throne when our Blessed Savior, at the Last Supper, joined with the disciples in singing the 118th Psalm. "And when they had sung an hymn, they went out into the mount of Olives" (Matthew 26:30 KJV).

Music is essentially linked with the emotions. What an important part melody and harmony in rhythm and note and tune and hymn and word, have played in human affairs throughout the world's history! The direct relation of music is not to ideas, but to feeling. Music does not sound the depths of knowledge--it fathoms the depths of the heart. The strains of martial music to the rhythm of marching troops do not convey the understanding of courage, but they do impart the gift of courage, inasmuch as they inspire the feelings of courage. The strains of:

"My country, 'tis of thee,
Sweet land of liberty
Of thee I sing;
Land where my fathers died,
Land of the pilgrims' pride,
From every mountainside,
Let freedom ring"

do not offer any elaborate definition of patriotism, but they quicken the heartbeat of every patriot to deeds of desperate daring in the interests of truth and liberty. Thus it is music has played throughout all time a great part in subduing passion, in nerving energy, in comforting sorrow and in evoking aspirations to the highest ideals. This truth was well understood by the ancient Greeks, for it was forbidden in their republic to play anything but warlike music, in order that the courage of their soldiers should not be weakened by softer and more pathetic influences.

At most crises in the history of nations a song arises that crystallizes the thought and aspirations of the people. The "Marseillaise" was the war cry of the French Revolution. It symbolized the aims of the people in that mighty struggle; it lives today as the concrete expression of the determination of a nation to achieve freedom. Our own loved national hymn, "The Star-Spangled Banner," was born amid the reek and smoke, the wounds and death of battle, when, after the bleeding struggle of Fort McHenry the American poet, through a burst of tears, in the solemnity of the dawn, saw that the Stars and Stripes was still flying over the beleaguered fort.

> "O say, can you see
> By the dawn's early light,
> What so proudly we hailed
> At the twilight's last gleaming,
> Whose broad stripes and bright stars,
> Through the perilous fight,
> O'er the ramparts we watched
> Were so gallantly streaming?
> And the rockets' red glare,
> The bombs bursting in air,
> Gave proof through the night
> That our flag was still there;
> O say, does that Star-Spangled Banner yet wave
> O'er the land of the free
> And the home of the brave?"

Music stirs latent powers, resurrects dead hopes, reawakens lost ambitions and brings to a determined purpose the soul which has lingered long in the valley of indecision. My father, the Founder, early recognized that the power of music is not nullified by lack of education. It appeals to the lowly and unlearned as well as to the high and tutored, and he realized that wise is the legislator who gives the art of music the greatest encouragement.

So from the commencement our first General made music a potent factor in his great plan for winning the people for God. The cornet and the drum were among our very first measures to attract the masses, and although at first they met with bitter opposition, and our early followers suffered almost every brutality because of their heroic persistence in their use, the persecution but made the attraction the greater. The divine purpose was soon recognized by all classes and all nations, and our Army bands have made such progress that today there is not an instrument of wind, of key, of pipe, of reed, of string, of parchment, of brass, of wood, of steel, or of bone, that has not been marshaled into the instrumental lines of our 43,000 bandsmen, who, in their sacrificial devotion to God and humanity, lift an unbroken note of salvation the whole world over.

The ember of the love of harmony amidst the ashes in the discordant hearts of the discouraged and the sinful has been fanned to a flame, when we have carried spiritual and patriotic music to the fetid slums, to the congested byways, to the prison cells and to the places of congregated vice and misery. Attracted by the shining brass, a quick march, or a well known tune, memories, long slumbering, have stirred and drunkards have left their drink, girls their hidden haunts of iniquity, mothers, weary, have forsaken their toils, little children have turned from their play to unite their tender voices. In every part of the world the ne'er-do-wells, the loafers, the dull of conscience, the dead of heart--all have followed on the sidewalks or beside the procession to keep within hearing of the strains lifted by tens of thousands of Salvation Army bandsmen. Salvation Army music has proved efficacious in drawing the attention of men to the demands of judgment; to the love of God; to the sacrifice of Christ.

Many of our brightest officers and our most devoted and trustworthy soldiers, who now fill high places of responsibility and confidence, were first attracted to our ranks and drawn to Christ by an Army band. Men of exceptional musical gifts have accepted the opportunities the Army offers to herald the tidings of the gospel by music, and have consecrated their talents to God under our flag.

The progress of our organization in instrumental craftsmanship can only be described as miraculous. There is no doubt that our early efforts, though enthusiastic, were not well directed. The results were sometimes more painful than pleasant to the listener. The musically educated jeered at our productions, but we kept right on. And God, the Author of all harmony, was with us. Today we have in our ranks some of the finest executants on their particular instrument as well as highly-gifted arrangers and composers. Our music takes a high place in the estimate of those competent to judge. Our festivals prove that the old story is outdated when one comrade said to the other, both being keen to become bandsmen:

> "Say, Bill, is it possible to be a good Christian and play the cornet?"
>
> To which Bill replied: "Sure! But it's mighty hard for the fellow next door to be one!"

I tell you there is no pen that can write, there are no words that can utter, the parchments of the skies can barely hold the story of the spiritual triumphs achieved by The Salvation Army bandsman. God bless him! God has blessed him! The Lamb's Book of Life alone records the struggles long and hard, in heat and in cold, in hidden places, in public squares--and the Lamb's Book of Life alone records the wounds healed, the sweet joy assured, the names written down through this day after day, year after year; persistent, whole-souled offering of ministry to Him who died for us, and to the world for whom He died.

* * * * *

I want now to speak especially to my own bandsmen in the United States of America. I think I have the right to do so. For that matter, I think I have a right to speak to our bandsmen all over the world.

Anyone whose career, from the years of a child, has been intermingled with bars, notes, clefs, ritards, crescendos, pianissimos, fortissimos, quavers, semi-quavers, demi-semi-quavers, tremolos--very much tremolo--as mine has been, has a right to speak.

Anyone who has with their own hands worked with concertinas, harps, pianos, banjos, snare drums, accordions and hand organs, and lastly and decidedly leastly cornets, has a right to speak.

Anyone who, because they have taken their allotted position in the brass band, has been arrested and roughly handled in the open streets as I have, has a right to speak.

Anyone who has carried the big drum down the broad thoroughfares of a fashionable city, with only a little lad to help with the load, while they beat it to the rhythm of a solo, the solo being the solitary voice of the drummer, as I have, has a right to speak.

Anyone who has patiently and unresistingly received the blows of the infuriated vicious--blows of bricks, sticks, stones and pieces of iron fender and pots and pans, while they endeavored to shield with their own body the smallest member of the band, a little drummer boy, as I have, has a right to speak.

Anyone who has stood in the witness box of the crowded courtroom and, with flushed cheeks and flying pulses successfully defended her comrade bandsmen under arrest, as I have, has a right to speak.

Anyone who has visited the House of Commons and House of Lords and, despite agonizing feelings of timidity, with trembling limbs but courageous lips presented to individual members of both Houses the biblical conviction of our call to "preach the gospel to the poor," and our individual commission from "the Judge of all the earth" to go "into the highways and byways," with the result of an overwhelming victory, as I have, has a right to speak.

Anyone who has knocked at as many doors and climbed as many steps and met as many rebuffs and smiled back at as many frowns, soliciting funds for brass instruments, as I have, has a right to speak.

Anyone who has seen their bandsmen comrades, in their brave struggle for liberty, knocked down at their feet and the blood spurt from their temples, as from a turned-on faucet, as I have, has a right to speak.

Anyone who has played on Highgate Hill, London, the snare drum on the condition that the large and select crowd only threw gold pieces into the collection, the amount according to the efficiency of the snare drummer's production, as I did, has a right to speak.

Anyone who, with lips naturally tremolo, shaking like a leaf in a storm, has reached the high standard of playing on the cornet in public the solo, "The Last Rose of Summer," starting in the triumph of an awakening bud and ending in the defeat of scattered petals, as I have, has a right to speak.

Anyone who has been the recipient of the wholehearted devotion, the close following, the ready obedience, the generous affection, the gallant protection and the heroic defense from Salvation Army bandsmen in England, in Canada and in this country as I have, has a right to speak.

Anyone who has that innate love of music for which the brass band has an exceptional fascination; whose pulses agitate, whose heart pounds, whose spirit beats within their breast as a bird's wings against its cage, at the martial strains of military music as mine does, has a right to speak. Lastly, anyone who was born upon that day when the band of the heavenly seraphim threw its songs across earth and sky--that day when organs and bells and trumpets and horns are chiming and pealing and thrilling the world with the tidings of the joy of the song of peace and good will, as I was, has a right to speak--and so I speak.

So I speak--and here is what I want to say to my bandsmen. First, second and lastly, never forget that whatever degree your musical gift may register--how high or low it may be--you have consecrated it to God. Your confession says so. The banner under which you march says so.

You have not taken your musical endowment and said, "I will use this for my own gain." You have laid it in the hands of Him who gave it, that it may be used for His glory. You have placed it, your offering, upon His altar. It is your share in His Kingdom. Possibly you did not possess wealth, or beauty, or other earthly equipment. This talent was your prized possession, your treasure, and it was your consecrated tribute to be laid at the feet of Christ. When you heard His voice saying, "Go and sell all that thou hast and give to the poor," that is just what you did. You gave what you had to give, that it might help carry to the poor the riches in Christ Jesus.

Doubtless you were young the first time your fingers found the valves of the cornet, or your lips the mouthpiece of the trombone; and as the years have passed the treasure given to God has increased in worth, and many times the devil has tempted you sorely to take back from the altar that which you laid upon it. But no! It is God's. You gave it to Him in sincerity and in truth. You gave it with tears in your eyes and a prayer in your heart that His Spirit would make it a holy offering, pure and acceptable in His sight, consecrated to His service, and that He would use it to help bring His Kingdom upon earth. To take it back is to rob God of His own.

Now I want to remind you that the irrevocable, unalterable, unchangeable condition of the continued usefulness of our offerings to God is holiness. Holiness consists of three great principles; separation from sin, abandonment to the will of God and a life fashioned in the likeness of Jesus Christ's. This is whiteness of word and thought and deed.

It is this behind the instrument; it is this exercised in the lives of a body of men that exerts a force, directs an influence and sends forth as with eagle flight a power that breaks the fascination of evil, lifts the weight of sorrow, assuages wicked passions and directs every heart upon which its message falls to the world's great Corrector of life's every discord.

Keep your offering holy--acceptable unto God. If in your personal life you fail to measure up to the standard your presence in The Salvation Army declares, then you are desecrating a high position in our ranks. You are enacting a great wrong to yourself, to your comrades, to the reputation of Salvation Army bandsmen in every part of the world, to the memory of the saints who in the hard struggle for liberty of the early days, in beatings and stonings, in prison cells and persecutions innumerable, by patience in suffering and whiteness of life hallowed the Army bandsman's uniform and immortalized His name.

My dear bandsmen, keep the offering holy and then, ten thousand hallelujahs, we shall support and multiply this irresistible force for God and goodness--The Salvation Army band.

Never forget, you are a part of a great whole. It makes no difference the instrument you play. The dimension of the tree is not always regulated by the size of the seed--so the results of our part cannot be estimated by their apparent importance.

The factor which should ever move us to our best should be that our part is good, is pure, is true, that the note of our personal and public life is in tune with the instrument of the Divine Master's will and in perfect accord with the Ten Commandments.

Again, do not forget that to you is given the greatest opportunity for helping others. Every time you go out in the open-air, every time you sound the clear, sweet notes of your instrument, or the heartbeat of the drum, all eyes are turned toward you--you cannot avoid being seen--you cannot avoid being heard--some eyes that rest upon you; some ears that listen to you; some lover of music whose dead heart thrills with life as he hears you; some little child who hastens home to tell mother about you; some old man who sees again his own youth presented in you; some bedridden soul who catches the strains of heavenly promises because of you; some thousands of sinners whose hard spirits melt and stony hearts break at the foot of the Cross listening to you, will one day--one day--the world's gladdest day--and Heaven's most musical day with every bell apeal and every harp aring and every voice asong, will rise up to call you blessed in the name of Him who is the leading note of all music-- Jesus.

Again, a large portion of Salvation Army bandsmen are young in years. That is, you have not yet reached the prime of life. You stand before the open gates of marvelous possibilities--possibilities of service to humanity.

You are the children of parents who were saved in the Army before you were born. Before you came into the world the prayer that rang through every chamber of your mother's and father's heart was that if spared you should be a true follower of Jesus Christ; that you should find your place in the ranks of the forces for righteousness in which they had fought. When you were only two, or four, or six years of age they carried you back and forth to the meeting as Hannah carried Samuel to the temple, so that in your awakening intelligence you might be imbued with holy influences. With what hope and loving faith they watched their little boy coming along the paths of childhood. Then their anxiety through the school days. With what tears and encouragement and warnings they helped you to resist evil, to despise the ignoble, to condemn trickery, to hate sin. How bright the vision with which they visualized you in manhood brave and strong and daring upon the fields of truth!

The greatest joy of your parents' life was when you made known to them that of your own volition, your choice was made and that it was for God and the Army. Mother burst into tears and took you in her arms just as she used to do when you were only a little fellow. Father patted you first on your head and then again and again on your shoulders as though he fain would place his hand upon your heart and leave it forever there.

Well, how has it been through the years? How is it with you in these latter days? There is nothing more beautiful than to see a young man living a life of purity; standing upright where thousands of the insincere and hypocritical fall down. What vistas of service open up before such a one! What high ambitions fire his soul! To his earthly eyesight is added spiritual vision. He sees not only the things of today. He realizes something of the great things God has awaiting him. Is this so with you? Are you satisfied with these duties--blessed as they are--which start and finish with your instrument? Or has God revealed to you the far wider field--yourself as a David striking down the enemies of men's souls and winning those souls for God?

Why should officers and other members of the corps feel it to be incumbent upon them to carry the responsibility of the spiritual life of the bandsman, and the bandsman not realize that standing in the front ranks of observation as his instrumental duties demand, he is in a very special sense obligated to God and to his comrades to keep a rigid watch upon his ways and ever strive that his life should be blameless before God and man? Young men I beg you fight for this. You will then find the shams in religion and the false, whoever and wherever they are, will seek others for their companions and you will move in honorable circles all the days of your life. Some old friends of your father's will meet you one day and say, "Why, my boy, how glad I am to see you! Just like your good, old father for all the world."

Let your Commander, who is your own fond leader and also is to you as a parent, warn you. Shun those who indulge in impure conversation. You take a step downward, when without resentment you allow anyone to tell you a story that is indecent in its suggestion. Better allow a man to strike you in the face than that he should have it to say you enjoyed with him a conversation that was impure and not in full support of your uniform. Again never permit an association with one whom you know to be violating the laws of our Salvation Army teachings of honor and truth.

If any offender attempts to entice you to indulge in tasting any form of forbidden fruit, remember who you are, the ten thousand prayers behind you and the ten thousand hopes stretching out into an endless eternity before you. Let your better nature assert itself and prove true to Salvation Army traditions--purity of life--never forgetting that "Blessed are the pure in heart, for they shall see God."

No sense of loyalty to a pal must induce you to play false to your God. Truth is the measure of your righteousness. Whatever is beside that, no matter by what consent authorized, or by what motive prompted, is a blow at the foundation upon which the entire moral structure rests. Without truth there is no correctness, and without correctness there is no beauty. There can be nothing correct without truth. The loveliest feature in the natural world is truth. True features make the beauty of a face, and true lines the beauty of architecture and true measures the beauty of music, and true words, true thoughts, true deeds the beauty of a life, and a true heart the beauty of every service and grace that springs from life.

If you condone a weakness or evil practice a comrade confides to you, you are playing false to him and breaking down every law of friendship.

Does anyone ask what to do in such a case?

In the first place, condemn the forbidden thing. Speak of it as it is in all its real hideousness, for all sin is hideous. Do your best to talk of it as your godly father would do. Point out the entanglements, evil consequences and backslidings that belong to it and persuade by every sacred bond of Salvationism and by every fond memory of comradeship--persuade the one concerned to abandon the wrong. Pray together and, as man struggling with man, help him to fight back the enemies of his soul. Lead him away from hypocrisy and death. If he refuses to forsake his evil ways, then you must cut the partnership and abandon him. There is no other way to save your own soul. The Bible says: "He that toucheth pitch shall be defiled therewith."

The dearest and truest friends are those who help us to overcome our weaknesses and triumph over our temptations.

Tone your life to prayer, to right thinking, to noble deeds. Be careful that your worship is not rejected because your heart is not in it. Keep away from all places and things of question and doubt. Remember "the cloud of witnesses." Look to the new Jerusalem, and the music of heavenly voices will sound in your soul.

An Italian made a chime of bells for his native village. So sweet was the chime that he built a little home close beside it that he might catch its every tone. After a while war came. The Italian was taken into exile, the bells were captured and were also taken away. Many years passed. One day the Italian exile, in a rowboat, is being rowed up the River Shannon, toward the City of Limerick, Ireland.

As he comes near the wharf the cathedral tower strikes the chime; and lo, it was the same old chime of bells that in other days enchanted him. He recognized them in a moment. His emotions were too great for human endurance. He folded his arms and lay back in the boat. The rowers put down their oars and tried to resuscitate him. His face was toward the tower. But he was gone. His soul had gone out in the raptures of that hour. His life fell under the stroke of the chime of Limerick Cathedral.

So may it be with us when going up from this earthly exile into the harbor of our God. May we fold our arms in peace and listen; and, while the rowers are taking us to anchorage, with our face toward the "high tower," from turret and dome, and palace gate and arch of eternal victory, may there come rippling upon our souls the chimes of the divine concord which the entire universe is destined one day to sound.